Max-Planck-Institut für ausländisches
öffentliches Recht und Völkerrecht

Beiträge zum ausländischen öffentlichen Recht und Völkerrecht

Begründet von Viktor Bruns

Herausgegeben von
Armin von Bogdandy · Rüdiger Wolfrum

Band 205

Rüdiger Wolfrum · Ulrike Deutsch (eds.)

The European Court of Human Rights Overwhelmed by Applications: Problems and Possible Solutions

International Workshop

Heidelberg, December 17–18, 2007

ISBN 978-3-540-93959-7   Springer Berlin · Heidelberg · New York

e-ISBN 978-3-540-93960-3   DOI 10.1007/978-3-540-93960-3

Beiträge zum ausländischen öffentlichen Recht und Völkerrecht   ISSN 0172-4770

Bibliografische Information der Deutschen Nationalbibliothek
Die Deutsche Nationalbibliothek verzeichnet diese Publikation in der Deutschen Nationalbibliografie; detaillierte bibliografische Daten sind im Internet über http://dnb.d-nb.de abrufbar.

© by Max-Planck-Gesellschaft zur Förderung der Wissenschaften e.V., to be exercised by Max-Planck-Institut für ausländisches öffentliches Recht und Völkerrecht, Heidelberg 2009

Dieses Werk ist urheberrechtlich geschützt. Die dadurch begründeten Rechte, insbesondere die der Übersetzung, des Nachdrucks, des Vortrags, der Entnahme von Abbildungen und Tabellen, der Funksendung, der Mikroverfilmung oder der Vervielfältigung auf anderen Wegen und der Speicherung in Datenverarbeitungsanlagen, bleiben, auch bei nur auszugsweiser Verwertung, vorbehalten. Eine Vervielfältigung dieses Werkes oder von Teilen dieses Werkes ist auch im Einzelfall nur in den Grenzen der gesetzlichen Bestimmungen des Urheberrechtsgesetzes der Bundesrepublik Deutschland vom 9. September 1965 in der jeweils geltenden Fassung zulässig. Sie ist grundsätzlich vergütungspflichtig. Zuwiderhandlungen unterliegen den Strafbestimmungen des Urheberrechtsgesetzes.

Die Wiedergabe von Gebrauchsnamen, Handelsnamen, Warenbezeichnungen usw. in diesem Werk berechtigt auch ohne besondere Kennzeichnung nicht zu der Annahme, dass solche Namen im Sinne der Warenzeichen- und Markenschutz-Gesetzgebung als frei zu betrachten wären und daher von jedermann benutzt werden dürften.

Einbandgestaltung: WMXDesign GmbH, Heidelberg

Gedruckt auf säurefreiem Papier

springer.de

Foreword

The European Court of Human Rights is faced with a huge and ever-growing workload. Up until 1998, the Court pronounced only 837 judgments, while it rendered 4.000 judgments in the last three years alone. On 18 September 2008, the European Court of Human Rights delivered its 10.000th judgment; currently, there are some 100.000 cases pending before the Court. This enormous caseload is both a testimony to the Court's success and of the considerable threat posed to the effectiveness of the protection of the rights and freedoms guaranteed by the European Convention on Human Rights and its Protocols. Moreover, Protocol No. 14, which was intended to alleviate the problem by increasing the efficiency of the Court, is still not in force.

This publication is intended to contribute to the ongoing discussion about the reforms that are necessary to prevent a failure of the European system of human rights protection. It compiles the contributions of a workshop which took place on 17-18 December 2007 at the Max Planck Institute for Comparative Public Law and International Law in Heidelberg and the discussions following the presentations. The convening of this workshop was recommended by Christian Tomuschat.

The conference brought together academics and practitioners and thus offered an excellent opportunity for the discussion of possible approaches to the dilemma. Christian Tomuschat's presentation outlined the success story of the European Court of Human Rights and the resulting danger of failure of the system and gave an overview of possible solutions. Rudolf Bernhardt concentrated on the merits of introducing a discretionary admission procedure and argued for a radical reform of the present system. Jochen Abr. Frowein focused on the need to introduce a filtering mechanism as part of the exhaustion of domestic remedies, which would consist of special chambers on the Supreme Court level of Member States for dealing with Convention cases. Luzius Wildhaber analysed the approach of the Court to issuing pilot judgments in cases concerning structural problems affecting a large number of persons. Finally, Mark Villiger took a close look at a particular group of cases responsible for the huge back-log, i.e., cases concerning the length of proceedings.

Our personal thanks go to Yvonne Klein and Falilou Saw in whose hands rested the entire organization of the workshop. We would also like to thank Dr. Christiane Philipp who was heavily involved in editing the manuscript. Furthermore, thanks are due to Verena Schaller-Soltau for her technical assistance.

Heidelberg, November 2008

Rüdiger Wolfrum

Table of Contents

The European Court of Human Rights Overwhelmed by
Applications: Problems and Possible Solutions 1
   Christian Tomuschat

Discussion Following the Presentation by Christian
Tomuschat 19

The Admissibility Stage: The Pros and Cons of a
Certiorari Procedure for Individual Applications 29
   Rudolf Bernhardt

Discussion Following the Presentation by Rudolf
Bernhardt 37

The Interaction Between National Protection of Human
Rights and the ECtHR 51
   Jochen Abr. Frowein

Discussion Following the Presentation by Jochen Abr.
Frowein 55

Pilot Judgments in Cases of Structural or Systemic
Problems on the National Level 69
   Luzius Wildhaber

Discussion Following the Presentation by Luzius
Wildhaber 77

Fair Trial and Excessive Length of Proceedings as Focal
Points of the ECtHR's Increasing Caseload 93
   Mark Villiger

Discussion Following the Presentation by Mark Villiger 103

Concluding Remarks 121
    Rüdiger Wolfrum

List of Participants 123

The European Court of Human Rights Overwhelmed by Applications: Problems and Possible Solutions

Christian Tomuschat

I. Introduction

Is it not an almost unbelievable success story? Currently, the jurisdiction of the European Court of Human Rights (ECtHR) extends to 47 States with more than 800 million inhabitants. Accordingly, international judges review the activities of 47 governments as to their compatibility with the European Convention on Human Rights (ECHR). No injusticiable areas or groups of acts exist. The ECtHR has abstained from evolving a doctrine of act of State or *acte de gouvernement*.[1] Everyone who feels aggrieved by a decision or some factual conduct of public authorities can bring the relevant dispute before the Strasbourg judges after having exhausted domestic remedies. Invariably, the case will be heard.[2] The Strasbourg Court has no discretion to accept or reject a case *a limine*. In 2006, it handed down no less than 1.560 full judgments. Thus, paradise in full blossom seems to have been ushered

---

[1] But see the Grand Chamber decision in *Markovic v. Italy*, application 1398/03, 14 December 2006, where the ECtHR had to assess a doctrine of *acte de gouvernement* evolved in Italy.

[2] This is the excruciating strength and weakness of the system of the ECHR, see Paul Mahoney, "Thinking a Small Unthinkable: Repatriating Reparation from the European Court of Human Rights to the National Legal Order", in Lucius Caflisch *et al.* (eds.), Liber Amicorum *Luzius Wildhaber: Human Rights – Strasbourg Views*, Kehl 2007, p. 263, at 267.

in. Can we therefore assume that the rule of law, as encapsulated in human rights, has found its definitive consecration in Europe?

II. The Growth of the Strasbourg System

Indeed, who would have thought, when the journey to the peak we have reached by now began in the late forties of the last century, that human rights in Europe would ever be based on such strong foundations? There is no need to dwell at length on the political and historical origins of the ECHR. I shall confine myself to mentioning some basic facts. After the horrors of the Nazi regime in Germany, the world community was generally agreed that any recurrence of a murderous dictatorship should be forestalled by all conceivable means. For that reason, the UN Charter defined the promotion and the encouragement of respect for human rights and fundamental freedoms as one of the primary purposes of the World Organization (Article 1 (3)). A few years later, on 10 December 1948, with a view to particularizing this general formula, the Universal Declaration of Human Rights was proclaimed. This Declaration served as a source of inspiration for the newly founded Council of Europe (the Statute of the Council of Europe entered into force on 3 August 1949). Taking the work which had already been performed by the UN Commission on Human Rights for a world covenant on human rights as the basis for its own drafting efforts, the Council of Europe succeeded in finalizing the draft text of the ECHR in the autumn of the next year. On 4 November 1950 the ECHR could be signed during a solemn ceremony in Rome. After having received the first ten ratifications, it entered into force on 3 September 1953. The UK had been the first State to accept the new instrument, but Germany was also among the pilot group of ten States who had the courage to bind themselves under the terms of an international regime the effects of which were unforeseeable at that time.

The first years saw a slow, but progressive enlargement of the circle of States parties. Especially the bigger States hesitated initially to follow the adventurers who had paved the way. While Turkey joined the group in May 1954, Italy took the decision not earlier than in October 1955. But it was France which adjourned its ratification for more than two decades. Although the ECtHR took its seat in Strasbourg, and although *René Cassin* was one of the first Presidents of the ECtHR (1965–1968), the French government waited until May 1974 before finally joining the

States that had manifested their confidence in the operation of the new regime by submitting to it. Apparently, France felt that as the country where the Déclaration des droits de l'homme et du citoyen had been proclaimed in 1789, in other words, as "la patrie des droits de l'homme", it had no ground to submit to international control its governmental conduct. In a country which had "invented" human rights, everything was fine by definition.

Until the great change in Europe, the number of parties to the ECHR remained at the level of 22 States. The demise of socialism as a political doctrine brought about by the political occurrences in 1989/90 entailed dramatic results and led eventually to a tremendous increase in membership to more than the double of the figures reached until then. The first State to become a member of the Council of Europe and thereafter to ratify the ECHR was Finland (10 May 1990), which during the reign of socialism in Eastern Europe had not dared to embark on the way to Strasbourg, out of fear to antagonize its great neighbour to the east, the Soviet Union. With some slight delay, taking a lot of precautions, the former satellites of the Soviet Union followed suit: the Czech Republic on 3 March 1992, Hungary on 5 November 1992, and Poland on 19 December 1993. Currently, all the Eastern European States have joined the family of nations grouped around the ECHR, with the sole exception of Belarus which, because of open disregard for the rule of law, being under the tight grip of a dictatorship, is currently still unfit for membership in the Council of Europe. It was a dramatic event when the former superpower itself, now under the name of Russia, was admitted to membership in the Council of Europe in February 1996 and thereafter ratified the ECHR in May 1998. It is not absolutely clear what objectives were pursued by Russia when it made that move to the west of the continent. One may presume that in 1996/98 Russia felt that in order to demonstrate its definitive rupture with its Stalinist past it should accept international obligations to respect and observe human rights. It must have felt politically weak, seeking to rehabilitate itself morally by cooperating with the other States of the continent on a level of parity, without enjoying any prerogatives. Indeed, within the Council of Europe, contrary to the configuration obtaining at the United Nations, the larger States have not been granted any special status, which, in principle, is acceptable even for more powerful countries since the Council of Europe has no true decision-making power.

However, such powers do exist under the regime of the ECHR. From the very outset, it was the particularity of the ECHR that it established not only a certain number of substantive guarantees but that it sought at the same time to make those guarantees truly effective by providing for enforcement machinery. It was an exceptionally bold decision to introduce an inter-State application by virtue of which every State party is entitled – and politically even called upon – to act as guardian of legality in instances where another State party is seen as breaching the provisions of the ECHR (formerly Article 24, now Article 33). This was a principled departure from the rule of consent which normally governs international dispute settlement: under general international law, reflected in Article 33 (1) of the UN Charter, States have the right of free choice regarding the way in which they wish to lay to rest any international disputes that they may have with another State. Here, by contrast, they accepted to be made accountable before the European Commission for any violation of the obligations incumbent upon them under the ECHR. The relevant provision can be seen as the precursor of what the ICJ, many years later, in its famous *Barcelona Traction* judgment, called 'obligations *erga omnes*'. The provision giving leave to challenge another State must be viewed as the expression of the idea that the ECHR as a whole protects common goods, the preservation of which lies in the public interest of the community of States assembled under the roof of the ECHR.

As everyone here knows, little use was made of the inter-State application. A couple of years ago, the Parliamentary Assembly invited the States parties to bring an application against Russia on account of the tragic occurrences in Chechnya,[3] but no government took up that challenge. Notwithstanding that reluctance to put into motion a procedure specifically designed for such occurrences,[4] one should not lose sight of the fundamental importance which the inter-State application holds as a matter of principle. The existence of this remedy underlines the position of the community of States parties as guarantors of the rights set forth by the ECHR. In practice, though, it has been more or less supplanted by the individual application which permits the victim of a violation directly to bring his/her case to the Strasbourg system, without having to prevail upon his/her home state to initiate a process of diplomatic protection.

Originally the individual application depended on a special declaration which every State party was free to make or not to make (Article 25). A

---

[3] Recommendation 1456 (2000), 6 April 2000, *HRLJ* 21 (2000) 286.

[4] On 27 March 2007, an application was filed by Georgia against Russia. It is still pending.

government could choose just to be bound by the substantive provisions of the ECHR without assuming at the same time the remedy of individual application. In this regard, progress was slow. The Scandinavian States Sweden, Denmark and Iceland, together with Ireland, took the lead. The acceptance of the individual application by both Belgium and Germany in July 1955 brought the procedure into force (Article 24 (4) required six declarations before it could be applied). Again, many of the bigger States had enormous difficulties in taking this second step which moved the ECHR to the top of all mechanisms of human rights protection world-wide. The United Kingdom waited for more than ten years before making its declaration under Article 25 on 14 January 1966. Italy came several years later, it followed suit in July 1973. Again, France was the last one of the big European nations to submit to the control mechanism of individual application. Only in October 1981, more than 30 years after the signature of the ECHR, did it take the step which Germany had taken a quarter of a century earlier.[5] Was it fear, was it arrogance, was it the mindset of sovereignty which prevented the French government from accepting the principle of international monitoring of its activities? In any event, it was a hard decision for it to take. Obviously, France needed a lot of time in order to get accustomed to the idea that the last word in a dispute was not spoken in Paris but in Strasbourg, and by an international body.

After France had eventually overcome its hesitations, the conviction spread that the split between accepting the ECHR as an instrument embodying substantive guarantees and rejecting its jurisdictional clauses had become outdated and could not be accepted any longer. Whoever takes a commitment to respect and observe human rights seriously must also be prepared to submit to international monitoring.[6] Eventually, only three States remained outside the jurisdiction of the ECtHR, namely Malta, Turkey and Cyprus. Pressure was increased on these three States. Bowing to that pressure, they made the requisite declarations. Turkey's declaration under Article 25 of 28 January 1987 was accompanied by far-reaching reservations through which Turkey sought to evade any accountability for the activities of its armed forces

---

[5] See Christian Autexier, "Frankreich und die EMRK nach der Unterwerfungserklärung (Art. 25) vom 2. Oktober 1981", *ZaöRV* 42 (1982) 327.

[6] See Luzius Wildhaber, "The European Convention on Human Rights and International Law", *ICLQ* 56 (2007) 217, at 222.

in Cyprus.[7] In 1989/90, at the time when the Berlin wall fell and thereby the artificial division of Europe into east and west, all of the then 22 States parties had finally made the declarations permitting individuals to file complaints and recognizing the jurisdiction of the Court at a second level after the Commission.

It was even more difficult to get the control machinery rolling. After the individual application had become applicable for six States in 1955, one might have expected that lawyers from those countries would not wait for a second to make use of the new legal opportunity offered to them. But that was not the case. In 1955, just 138 applications were registered, and this number decreased over the next years: in 1956 only 104 applications were filed, 101 in 1957, and 1958 reached a low point with no more than 96 applications. It was not so much ignorance on the part of lawyers which explains this drop. On the contrary, the legal profession noted with great attention that the European Commission conceived of its role as being that of a defender of governmental interests, to put it drastically. With stubborn rigidity, initially it rejected all incoming applications as being inadmissible, basing itself largely on the criterion of "manifestly ill-founded". The Strasbourg system appeared to be just an artificial construction, not really caring for the common man. Since the Commission swept any complaints away, there was not even any need for the Court that was to commence its activity after eight States would have recognized its jurisdiction. Only in 1959 did the Court come into being, and it could hand down its first judgment on 14 November 1960 in the case of *Lawless*. After having rejected the preliminary objections raised by the respondent, the government of Ireland, it pronounced its first judgment on the merits of that case on 1 July 1961.

But this was by no means the great breakthrough which the elected judges had hoped for. In the second case, a case against Belgium (*De Becker*), the Court could only note that the case had become moot as a consequence of a number of measures taken by the Belgian authorities with a view to rehabilitating the complainant who had been sanctioned for collaboration with the German occupation forces during World War

---

[7] For a comment see Christian Tomuschat, "Turkey's Declaration under Article 25 of the European Convention on Human Rights", in *Progress in the Spirit of Human Rights. Festschrift für Felix Ermacora*, Kehl et al. 1988, p. 119. In its judgment of 23 March 1995 in *Loizidou v. Turkey (Preliminary Objections)*, A 310, p. 34, the Court declared Turkey's restrictions to its declarations under Articles 25 and 46 of the Convention to be invalid.

II (judgment of 27 March 1962). Then there was again a long interval for many years. In 1967 and 1968, the Court delivered its judgments on admissibility and merits in its third case, the *Belgian Linguistic* cases, where it came to the conclusion that Belgium had breached the principle of non-discrimination in regard to the right to education by not allowing certain children, on the basis of the residence of their parents, to have access to the French-language schools existing in six communes on the periphery of Brussels. By the end of the sixties, the Court had pronounced judgment in four other cases (*Wemhoff, Neumeister, Stögmüller, Matznetter*). On the whole, this harvest for an entire decade was disappointingly low.

Obviously, a new approach was necessary. The Commission had to understand that it was not tasked with fending off as many applications as possible, but to provide a forum for persons who could plausibly contend that their rights had been breached by their national authorities. Furthermore, it also had to understand that its mandate was essentially to pre-screen the registered applications but that defining determinations on the construction of the ECHR should be left to the Court. It was unacceptable that the Commission, by making wide use of its power to reject applications as being manifestly ill-founded, assumed the role of the pivotal body that decides on the great orientations to be followed in interpreting the ECHR. In the seventies, while *Jochen Frowein* was a member of the Commission, this new spirit progressively gained ground in that body. More applications were declared admissible, and more applications were eventually sent to the Court. Thus, the number of judgments rose steadily. In the last year before the fundamental reform of the system came into force (1997), involving the abolition of the Commission and the inclusion of the individual application in the regular treaty obligations which need no special acceptance and to which no reservation can be made, the Commission received 14.166 applications, 703 of which were declared admissible, and the Court handed down 106 judgments. That was really a maximum of what could be achieved with a Court composed of part-time judges who received no regular salary from the Council of Europe, but only a *per diem* for the days of their presence in Strasbourg.

It stands to reason that the new arrivals from Eastern Europe changed the picture profoundly. Although in all the former communist States new constitutions were enacted, their traditions and the mental structures of many of the leading politicians had been shaped by 45 years of the dictatorship of a political party. Therefore, to embrace the rule of law as the decisive yardstick in handling public affairs amounted to a political and also intellectual revolution. In order not to fall back into the unfortunate situation of split acceptance of the ECHR as to its substantive and procedural parts, a political agreement was concluded with all the candidates wishing to join the Council of Europe: after a short period they would have to ratify the ECHR, making at the same time the declarations under Articles 25 and 64. This strategy proved indeed successful. Only in the case of Russia there was a longer interval of more than two years between accession to the Council of Europe (28 February 1996) and its ratification of the ECHR (5 May 1998). With the advent of the 11th Protocol (1 November 1998), the option to shun the individual communication disappeared even formally. The alternative was clear. One could either become a State party to the ECHR, or one could remain aloof from it. The middle-ground was abandoned. No compromises were tolerated any longer. The alternative was: either yes or no.

III. The Control Machinery of the ECHR – Through its Successes on the Brink of Failure

To unite all the States of Europe under the roof of the Council of Europe was a great achievement. Today, this seems almost natural. But it was not. It is true that Eastern Europe lay in intellectual ruins. There were no firm national constitutional traditions that could have guided the countries liberated from the yoke of socialist dictatorship into the uncertain future. The value system that was embodied in the ECHR and had been further strengthened over the years by the work of the two monitoring institutions, the Commission and the Court, seemed to constitute the only constitutional philosophy that could be relied upon in building democratic institutions in consonance with the wishes of the peoples. Indeed, the logic of the ECHR can be described as aiming at the creation of a common constitutional space deeply permeated by the rights and freedoms enunciated by it.

In this regard, the control machinery provided for by the ECHR, which by now comprises only two organs, the Court and the Committee of Ministers, constitutes an indispensable element. Just the jurisprudence evolved by the Court evinces the necessity of a supervisory mechanism. National judges do assist in enforcing the rights under the ECHR. In recent times, the Court has even insisted on the necessity of preventive procedures at national level. The Court does not stick with the customary principle according to which the implementation of international commitments falls within national jurisdiction. Rightly, the Court emphasizes Article 13, which enjoins States to put at the disposal of everyone whose rights may have been violated, an "effective remedy", which means in fact that essentially defects should, to the extent possible, be ironed out at national level so that seizure of the Court becomes unnecessary. But it is unrealistic to assume that the highest national courts could make supervision by the Court redundant. International judges have a different outlook. They are not imprisoned in the thinking habits of a particular national school of reasoning. In particular, they are able to compare the practices of different countries in order to ascertain what is not only legal, but also practicable.

On the other hand, it is trivial to note that the European control machinery functions best if little is to be corrected, if the requisite review processes are activated at national level. Without being a chauvinist, one can say that Germany is particularly successful with the institutional arrangement it has put into place. On the one hand, the ECHR is part and parcel of the law applicable in Germany. On the other hand, the special remedy of constitutional complaint (*Verfassungsbeschwerde*) is well suited to address complaints against governmental conduct. It need not be explained here that the rights under the ECHR and the fundamental rights under the German Basic Law run largely parallel to one another. Consequently, if a person alleges that basic rights have been infringed such allegation implies mostly also the allegation that the corresponding guarantee of the ECHR has been breached. Since the political philosophy of the German Constitutional Court is not different from the general political approach of the ECtHR to the cases brought before it, the Constitutional Court will normally be able to sort out any major inconsistencies between the law and the practice governed by it. Concrete figures show that indeed the balance sheet of Germany is quite a favourable one. At first glance, this does not emerge very clearly. As of 31 December 2006, there were no less than 3.950 pending cases against Germany, and 2.217 new cases were lodged during 2006. But only eight cases were declared admissible, and the number of convictions, where a violation was found, was even lower: just six cases. The conclusion to be drawn is obvious: many people see Strasbourg as a kind of *ultima ratio* which they will in any event resort to after their efforts to vindicate the rights which they believe to hold have proved of no avail before German courts. Most of the time, criticism of the Court with regard to Germany concerns inability to comply with the rule that proceedings should be brought to a speedy end.

With regard to Switzerland, the ratio between cases handled and final pronouncements by the Court is slightly less favourable. In 2006, remaining also within the last year of reference for which specific data is available, saw 335 applications lodged. Five applications were declared admissible, and in nine cases the Court found a violation. A perusal of those cases leads to the conclusion that no structural deficiencies have emerged. Here and there problems came to light, even problems related to freedom of expression. But on the whole Switzerland has again confirmed its fine reputation of a country that remains firmly attached to the rule of law.

The diagnosis is more dramatic mainly with regard to the new States parties from Eastern Europe. The number of new applications is almost frightening. Again in 2006, Russia topped the list with 12.241 applications, followed by Romania with 4.878, and Poland which has added 4.646 new cases to the roll of the Court. At the end of last year, Russia had 19.300 pending cases, Poland 5.100, and Romania 10.850. But there are also 9.000 cases from Turkey waiting to be adjudicated, 4.300 from France and 3.400 from Italy. These figures show that it is not only the "new" States that face serious problems, but also those which since decades have been associated with the work of the Court. Nonetheless, the conclusion seems to be warranted that the centre of gravity of the ECHR has shifted towards Eastern Europe. As indicated by the figures just mentioned, much remains to be done to put the house in order, to achieve more than only semantic congruence with the requirements of the ECHR.

The weight of this workload is tremendous. One should congratulate the judges currently in office for having accepted their mandates and working hard to address the mass of human misery that has been placed before them, without losing courage. It is clear that without the effective assistance of the Court's staff[8] their battle would be lost from the very outset. But notwithstanding that valuable support, the mountain seems to grow in a way which nobody really knows how to manage

---

[8] On the legal configuration of the staff see Norbert Engel, "Status, Ausstattung und Personalhoheit des Inter-Amerikanischen und des Europäischen Gerichtshofs für Menschenrechte. Facetten und Wirkungen des institutionellen Rahmens", *EuGRZ* 30 (2003) 122 *et seq.*; Erik Fribergh, "The Authority over the Court's Registry within the Council of Europe", in Liber Amicorum *Luzius Wildhaber* (above n. 2), p. 145; Paul Mahoney, "Separation of powers in the Council of Europe. The status of the European Court of Human Rights vis-à-vis the authorities of the Council of Europe", *HRLJ* 24 (2003) 152 *et seq.*

any longer, despite all the efforts deployed by the judges and their staff. While, as I told a few minutes ago, in the early days the Court was happy to see a case generously attributed to it by the Commission, it handed down 107 judgments before the great reform in 1997. Numbers jumped quickly up to 889 judgments in 2001, 1.105 judgments in 2005 and 1.560 full judgments in 2006. Counting 300 workdays per year, this means that on average 5.2 judgments were pronounced per day. And the provisional statistics for 2007, which bring the data up to 30 November 2007, inform the reader that until that date 1.649 judgments had already been handed down. Thus, quite a significant additional number can be expected before the end of the year – the result of a work discipline which can hardly be surpassed. In sober mathematical figures this amounts to an increase of roughly 20 per cent from one year to the next.

One should not expect that this acceleration can be continued *ad infinitum*. Gross rates of 20 per cent cannot easily be repeated. And even more: such increases in productivity are not even desirable. Each case requires sufficient attention. In particular, the specificities of a particular set of facts should not be disregarded. It may well be that by standardizing the legal reasons given by the Court things could be dealt with even faster. But the danger is that then the actual case at hand gets out of sight, that essential details are overlooked. The Court is of course well-advised to rely on the assistance which is provided by its staff. Eventually, however, the personal responsibility of the judges must remain the key element of the adjudicatory process. It would be unacceptable – and even immoral – to transfer the assessment to be carried out almost in its entirety to the staff people in the service of the Court. Judges must have the time to familiarize themselves with the cases placed before them. It would be unacceptable to see their role confined to signing a product ready-made by their support services. The judges are elected by the Parliamentary Assembly. They are the people in whom trust resides, not the bureaucrats in the Registry, no matter how able and zealous they are.

But the situation as it obtains today is indeed alarming. While at the end of 2006, just one year ago, the number of pending cases had risen to nearly 90.000, the data made public for the first eleven months of the current year show that the symbolic borderline of 100.000 cases has now been crossed. On 30 November, less than three weeks ago, the number of pending cases had risen to 103.950.

This figure invites the reader to proceed to a few fairly simple calculations. In 2006, the record-breaking year, the number of full judgments, which addressed the complaints of the applicant extensively, either on admissibility, or on the merits, or on both, stood at 1.560, as already mentioned. Additionally, 28.160 cases were disposed of by judicial decision, i.e. by decisions declaring an application inadmissible or striking it out of the list. Lastly, 12.251 cases were dealt with administratively by the Registry in cases, above all, where the applicant either did not submit the necessary basic information or where the case was not actively pursued. Adding these figures, one obtains a sum of roughly 42.000 cases, which, under the current circumstances, may be regarded as the maximum that can be reached. This means that the Court, in spite of increasing its output, has a structural backlog of 2 ½ years to tackle. The average case will inevitably sit in the archives for 30 months before it can be touched.

This is a deplorable situation. The English adage: justice delayed is justice denied, is well-known. It is not just a light, ephemeral proposition, having no real significance. It plays a major role in the Court's work. Its agenda is packed with tens of thousands of cases in which judges did not comply with their duties or were overburdened because of neglect on the part of the authorities responsible for the provision of logistics and manpower.[9] Should the Court itself become unable to live up to the standard it requires to comply with from the domestic courts under its supervision, it would soon lose its well-deserved reputation. In fact, for people in quite a number of countries, and principally in countries of Eastern Europe, the Court has become a symbol of hope. Justice they could not get from their own courts because of systemic disturbances within the judicial system of their home country they hope to get from Strasbourg. And in fact, Strasbourg has not disillusioned them. As far as my personal knowledge goes, the European judges have never bowed before governmental authority, putting the *raison d'Etat* ahead of the defence of human rights. Many writers have attacked the *Bankovic* decision as such a departure from the correct path of the law. But in that case the Court did not yield to the pressure of NATO and/or its European members. It made clear that jurisdiction is something else than factual contact; this is the solid consideration upon which the *Bankovic* decision rests.[10] And future cases will show, I have no doubt about that,

---

[9] See Andrea Gattini, "Mass Claims at the European Court of Human Rights", in Liber amicorum *Luzius Wildhaber* (above n. 2), p. 271, at 274.

[10] See also Lucius Caflisch and Antonio A. Cançado Trindade, "Les conventions américaine et européenne des droits de l'homme et le droit international général', *RGDIP* 108 (2004) 5, at 36; Wildhaber (above n. 6), p. 223.

that *Bankovic* has a limited scope only. One example in particular comes easily to mind: once a person is in the custody of the armed forces of anyone State party, and therefore committed to its care, wherever that may be, inside or outside the territory of the 47 States parties, the Court will unequivocally affirm the responsibility of that State. Mistreatment during custody, in particular, will never escape the censure of the Court.

IV. Improving the Control Machinery

We are assembled here to reflect on possible remedies. The Court itself, first under President *Wildhaber*, now under President *Costa*, has done whatever is feasible. The judges cannot be blamed, on the contrary, they deserve praise. It is now incumbent on politicians to evolve a new strategy. But they need advice from the scholarly community, notwithstanding their intimate knowledge of the inner workings of the Council of Europe where ministerial delegates are involved, in particular, in supervising the execution of the judgments rendered – which can be a struggle almost as challenging as the assessment of an application.

1) One of the most obvious remedies is the ratification of Protocol No. 14, which would allow the adjudication of the merits of so-called "repetitive cases" where a "well-established case law of the Court exists". This particular procedure could bring an enormous gain of time, if handled intelligently, without harming the individual applicant. Furthermore, Protocol No. 14 would permit the entry onto the European stage of the single Judge, a figure which is known from domestic legal systems mostly from the lowest level. *Le juge de paix – voilà* the resemblance. The single Judge formation, as the text says, does have its problematic side. Of course, the single Judge will be confined to declaring an application inadmissible or striking it off the list of cases if this is possible without any further examination. In that regard, recommendations will be made by rapporteurs functioning under the authority of the President of the Court. Other than *Monsieur le juge de paix*, the single Judge will thus not be alone. He will be advised. I therefore take it that no such unfortunate developments will ever take place as they were reported from the working group of the UN-Subcommission on the Promotion and Protection of Human Rights tasked with pre-screening complaints under ECOSOC-Resolution 1503 (XLVIII). In that body, composed of five persons from the five regions acknowledged in the

World Organization, decisions were generally taken according to a lager mentality. Anything that could have political overtones was simply declared inadmissible by a majority of three members. However, it should simply be recalled that the system envisioned in Protocol No. 14 would be workable only as long as the single Judge acts in full impartiality, not being led by considerations of enmity or friendship. Currently, this would certainly be the case. Thus, no serious obstacles stand in the way of the single Judge – except for the fact that Russia stubbornly refuses to ratify the Protocol. There seems to be no real possibility to overcome its reluctance. Hence, realistically, one cannot reckon with the coming into force of the Protocol as long as the current tensions between the Russian government and the other governments of the States parties persist.

2) Could or should we increase the number of judges by just doubling them? The result would be 94 European judges – as compared to the nine judges of the US Supreme Court, for instance. This would look fairly odd – although it would not be that odd, after all. It is true that most national supreme courts are fairly lean bodies. But most of them are protected from becoming over flooded by rigid provisions on leave to appeal. Within domestic legal systems, not everyone has access to the highest judicial body. Some lower court must have granted a specific authorization – or it is the Supreme Court itself which selects the cases deserving to be reviewed at the highest level. Such procedures do not exist in Strasbourg. Professor *Bernhardt* will talk about the intrinsic worth of a *certiorari* procedure as it exists in the United States. In any event, the open gates of the ECtHR have entailed a workload which no other comparable institution has to shoulder. Comparisons with the US Supreme Court are therefore quite inappropriate. For a legal community of more than 800 million people, from which tens of thousands of applications will be received each year on a regular basis, 94 judges would certainly not be disproportionate. Still, the idea of having 94 judges creates a certain malaise. Above all, it would become extremely difficult to ensure the unity of the case law. In the long run, however, it may become inevitable to provide for such a tremendous increase in numbers, which, objectively, is not excessive either if compared with the number of judges operating at the highest level of just one country. In Germany, for instance, the Constitutional Court comprises 16 judges. Additionally, Germany has five more specialized supreme courts, each one with several chambers. Two German judges at the highest level, the European level, would therefore not be a luxury, and the additional expenditure would be minimal.

3) Limiting access to the ECtHR and confining its role to rendering judgments on key issues with far-reaching consequences[11] cannot be the ideal solution either. First of all, the Strasbourg judgments do not exist in the national languages of all of the 47 States parties to the ECHR. This makes them inaccessible to many of the domestic European judges, in spite of the saying that English has become the common language of our societies. One simply has to acknowledge the fact that many national judges are unable to read a legal document in the English (or the French) language. This is not only a technical problem, but affects very badly the authority of the judgments, which in the eyes of the *juge de paix* in Albania or Azerbaijan, or even in the German province, seem to pertain to a different world, a world far removed from their daily experiences.[12]

More generally, there are other structural grounds as well implying that the Strasbourg Court cannot have the same authority as a supreme court within a national system. In France or in Germany, for instance, one may safely assume that a decision rendered by such a court will not only become known to all of the lower tribunals, but that it will also be heeded in the future. Notwithstanding their judicial independence, lower judges will normally follow the jurisprudence of the superior echelons of the judicial hierarchy, mainly out of fear to see their decisions reversed in case they pursue a different line. The ECtHR is much more remote from the national judges. Their reluctance to adopt the propositions evolved by the Court may even receive some support from national governments. Therefore, if the Court is really meant to help the victims of injustices, it must necessarily address the factual substance of individual cases. Its general guidelines alone do not have the necessary impact.[13] No judgment from Strasbourg will really penetrate the wide plains of Siberia – to put it somewhat polemically. But it

---

[11] As suggested by Luzius Wildhaber, "A Constitutional Future for the European Court of Human Rights?", *HRLJ* 23 (2002) 161, at 164. The Group of Wise Persons, entrusted with making reform proposals, withdrew its suggestion to render "judgments of principle", made in its Interim Report, 3 May 2003, *HRLJ* 27 (2006), 274, at 278, paras. 50-51, in its Final Report, 15 November 2006, *HRLJ* 27 (2006), 279, at 284, paras. 69-69.

[12] Highlighted also in the Final Report of the Group of Wise Persons (above n. 11), 284, para. 71.

[13] Christian Tomuschat, "Individueller Rechtsschutz: das Herzstück des 'Ordre public européen' nach der Europäischen Menschenrechtskonvention", *EuGRZ* 30 (2003) 95 *et seq.*

is certainly true that the calculation of full reparation for injury suffered could be left to national judicial systems – which would save an enormous amount of time.[14]

4) Could one re-delegate a great part of the bulk currently being handled by Strasbourg to the supreme courts of the States parties? It is certainly worthwhile testing this modality, which would be in line with the tendency of the Court to render pilot judgments.[15] An appeal to the highest court(s) should be opened to everyone claiming that his/her rights under the ECHR have been violated.[16] In Germany, the controversial decision of the Constitutional Court in the *Görgülü* case acknowledges, notwithstanding its somewhat strange insistence on German sovereignty, that disregard of the guarantees of the ECHR could amount to a violation of the fundamental rights under the Basic Law.[17] If made the guardians of the ECHR, the highest national courts would follow the jurisprudence of the Strasbourg Court with the greatest attention. They would become valuable interlocutors who could enter into a constructive dialogue with their partner from the Council of Europe. But it is clear that the way to the highest national courts should not bar the way to Strasbourg, *inter alia* because to file an application there is cost-free and does not require the services of a lawyer. It is evident that careful coordination with domestic legal procedures would be necessary.

V. Concluding Observations

It is our personal view that governments in Western Europe have not yet become sufficiently aware of the inappreciable contribution of the

---

[14] See Mahoney (above n. 2), 279 *et seq.*

[15] The first pilot judgment was rendered in *Broniowski v. Poland*, application 31443/96, 22 June 2004, *HRLJ* 25 (2004), 23. For a comment see Lech Garlicki, "Broniowski and After: On the Dual Nature of 'Pilot Judgments'", in Liber Amicorum *Luzius Wildhaber* (above n. 2), 177; Vladimiro Zagrebelsky, "Questions autour de Broniowski", ibid. 521; Gattini (above n. 9), *passim*.

[16] The Group of Wise Persons (above n. 11) focused mainly on remedies lying in case of excessive length of proceedings, but eventually made a comprehensive recommendation to that effect (p. 288, para. 136).

[17] 111 *Entscheidungen des Bundesverfassungsgerichts* 307, at 323; English translation: *HRLJ* 25 (2004) 99, at 105-6.

ECtHR to the establishment and strengthening of a common European culture of democracy, human rights and the rule of law. Many see the work carried out in Strasbourg as just one of the facets within the vast array of international expert bodies as they have sprung up in recent years. Such lack of attention, which eventually translates into insufficient funding, is a big mistake. Undeniably, the ECHR together with its enforcement machinery has grown up in the climate of the liberal State of the Western constitutional civilization. The former socialist States of Eastern Europe are today full members of that constitutional network, on a level of parity and without any discrimination. Their status as equals is reflected, in particular, by their right to participate in the development of the Strasbourg system through judges of their nationality. Every State party has the right to nominate one lawyer for the discharge of that important task. And yet, it can be said that the groundwork had already been laid when the former socialist nations acceded to the ECHR. The principles and concepts which determine the jurisprudence of the Court were defined in the formative years of the seventies, eighties and nineties of the last century. As far as my knowledge goes, there was never any explicit talk of the *"acquis de Strasbourg"* while the European Communities branded the banner of *"acquis communautaire"* continually while they were engaged in negotiations on further enlargement. In the accession treaties, acceptance of the *"acquis communautaire"* was made a formal condition of accession. In fact, however, with regard to the ECHR exactly the same occurred. The new States could not seriously hope to escape the influence of the established case law. Today, the new judges all have the right to introduce their specific ideas and concepts into the process of construction of the ECHR. But the main structures of that edifice were already in existence when they joined the ECHR.

This seems to be particularly important with regard to Russia. The domestic constitution of Russia is a wonderful instrument, which satisfies all the needs of a hasty reader. Human rights, division of powers, constitutional court – everything is on display. But it is mostly just on display. Some of it works in practice. Yet, whenever strong political elements come into play, the system operates in consonance with the factual strength of the actors involved. The ECHR, on the other hand, cannot be marginalized as easily. No one of the States parties to it can unilaterally determine their scope and contents. Through its decisions on individual cases, the ECtHR has a strong impact on developments in Russia. That impact, unfortunately, does not seem to go beyond the individual case that has been adjudicated. Although the Court has made it clear that States have to take general measures in case it has emerged that some systemic deficiency exists, that effect of Articles 41 and 46 has not yet materialized as it should do. In any event, however, through its work, the Court is involved in a continual process of raising the level of constitutional culture in Russia and also in the other Eastern European States that currently have to struggle with hard problems, as reflected in the statistics with which I have confronted you. This is a far smoother process than the "dialogue" between politicians which more often than not falls on deaf ears.

The Western nations have a tremendous interest in seeing this process continue, inasmuch as it has no patronizing elements and permits Russian actors to participate actively in remedying any inconsistencies found. Just for this reason, they should shed their reluctance to provide substantial financing to the Strasbourg system. No investment may be as profitable in the long run. It is precisely the experience of European integration that peace and understanding can best be promoted by together conceiving and carrying out a common project. To make the rights under the ECHR a living reality is such a common project. Any effort should be made to ensure that the journey that was commenced together can be continued together.

Discussion Following the Presentation by Christian Tomuschat

L. Wildhaber: Just a few words on the Court's workload and backlog, which *Paul Mahoney* has recently qualified as "unmanageable". Indeed, the Court expects for the year of 2007 53.500 applications, it has 104.000 applications pending before it, 10.000 of which have been pending for more than 3 years and therefore constitute backlog. After 2 audit reports and a management report, we know that the Court is well managed, is productive and has streamlined its procedures again and again. All easy solutions have already been found.

Now every choice is difficult. Doing nothing will unavoidably be very difficult indeed in the long run. The audit reports have found that for the Court to cope with it would need 660 additional registry posts (at present there are 580 posts), i.e. more or less double the budget. That is not feasible politically. Even if the Court got all this money, I am less than sure that a mammoth court would be such a good idea. If it became known that applications could be handled within a year or less, I confidently forecast an avalanche of tens of thousands of new cases from all the new Member States in which citizens have no trust in national courts.

Let us therefore forget the idea of the double budget. What then? I begin by saying that the Russian refusal to ratify Protocol No. 14 has had a chilling effect on all reform attempts. Apart from that, there is not only Russia's resistance, but also the even stronger resistance of a motley group of self-styled "friends of the applicants and perhaps also friends of the Court". This group, composed of NGOs, academics and even a minority of judges, believes that they are principled and everybody else is pragmatic, and that they will not allow the right of individual petition to be cut down. They have unfortunately been extremely successful. Protocols Nos. 11 and 14, the Management Report of Lord Woolf and the recent Report of the Group of Wise Persons have all tinkered with short-term considerations and have largely accepted the ideology which I just described, that discussion of the Court's workload situation and of the insidious undermining of the Court's credibility must be refused at all costs. "It would break my heart", said one of our judges, despite having been voted down by a clear majority of the judges repeatedly, "if I could not decide on all sorts of individual petitions". Of course, this is precisely what the Court cannot do. It rapidly accumulates new cases which will not be decided without massive delay, and the delays get steadily longer. Is that what is meant with the claim that the right of individual petition must not be touched?

Did you know, incidentally, that there were arguments that the Court could not cope with all its cases, that this proved that the Court was managed badly, and that therefore its budget should be cut? Given the situation which I just described, there will hardly be any meaningful reform in the near future, if there will be any reform at all. There will not be a massive expansion in the Court's budget. I grant that the Court itself could be more stringent when deciding on admissibility conditions, but again that will not happen easily, if it happens at all. One will have to be profoundly sceptical whether the "friends of the applicants" in their ideological rigidity will ever want to be also "friends of the Court", although I would want to remind everybody that there is no alternative to the Court. To the viewpoint of the NGOs that one cannot accept the world as it is and that one wants a better one, I would comment: who wouldn't want a better world, anyway?

E. de Wet: I would like to raise two questions. The first question relates to the fact that after the entering into force of the ECHR, several smaller States accepted the individual complaints procedure either immediately or very soon after ratification. This included countries like the Netherlands, which does not provide for constitutional review on the domestic level. However, this early embrace of the individual complaints procedure was not necessarily a reflection of an understanding of and commitment to the obligations contained in the ECHR at the time. In the Netherlands, for example, there was a general assumption at the time that the domestic laws and practices were already in accordance with the ECHR and that the country therefore had nothing to fear from the individual complaints procedure. It was only since the 1980s, notably after *Marckx v. Belgium*, that the Dutch legal establishment realized the potential impact of the ECHR on the Dutch legal system. My question therefore is whether the reluctance of States that initially refrained from accepting the individual complaints procedure was indeed or exclusively related to fears of diminished State sovereignty. Perhaps it also reflected a desire to first bring the national legal systems in harmony with the ECHR, in order to prevent a large number of complaints in Strasbourg.

If one applies this reasoning to the new Member States which have joined the Council of Europe in the 1990s, one could question the wisdom of early ratification (including of the individual complaints procedure). Had some of these States – with the support of the Council of Europe – attempted to bring their legal systems in accordance with the obligations under the ECHR *before* ratification, it might have prevented or limited the avalanche of cases with which the ECtHR is currently confronted.

The second question relates to Professor *Tomuschat's* reference to the *Bankovic* decision and the suggestion that the ECtHR is not inclined to bow to political pressure from Member States. One could question whether this really is the case, as the *Behrami and Saramati* decision may suggest otherwise. The manner in which the ECtHR attributed responsibility for the actions of KFOR exclusively to the United Nations is unconvincing. The delegation model on which the ECtHR relied acknowledges that the overall control exercised by the Security Council over the mandate of KFOR does not exclude effective control by the (Member States of) KFOR on the ground. If one regards attribution of responsibility and delegation of powers as two sides of the same coin (which the ECtHR seemed to do), the attribution of responsibility should reflect the fact that the (Member States of) KFOR were exercising effective control in Kosovo at the time that the alleged ECHR violation occurred. This would imply that responsibility for violations of the ECHR should first and foremost be attributed to the (Member States of) KFOR as opposed to the United Nations. This position is supported by United Nations practice, as the organisation has never before accepted responsibility for violations of international law by troops acting on its authority but under unified command and control (as is the case with KFOR). This means that the *Behrami and Saramati* decision results in an accountability vacuum, as the Member States are absolved from responsibility in a situation where no other entity is likely to assume responsibility. It has been alleged that the ECtHR's decision to attribute the responsibility for KFOR's actions exclusively to the United Nations resulted in part from political pressure exercised by those Member States that also constituted troop contributing States in Kosovo. If this were the case, it would indeed be a very worrying phenomenon.

M. Villiger: May I add an historical element to the presentation by Professor *Tomuschat*. Why did the number of applications at the outset remain stable and only later pick up? Professor *Tomuschat* mentioned the "Frowein Commission". Certainly, Professor *Frowein* brought in modern theories, modern views on human rights. He maintained rigorous standards of thought. But I think laurels should also go to the British lawyers. In the 1950s and in the 1960s, up to 50 per cent of the applicants were detained and 5 per cent were represented by lawyers. The scornful remark which the old Commission would hear would be: "you and your detainees"! This changed when British lawyers at the end of the 1960s and in the 1970s discovered the Convention, when they realized that the Commission's report and the Court's judgment could be a valuable tool in implementing their clients' rights in the domestic sphere. With their polished, at times brilliant presentations in often spectacular cases, they drew the attention of other lawyers to the Strasbourg complaints system. And lawyers no longer invoked only Article 5, but all substantive provisions of the Convention. Suddenly, the Convention became respectable and more and more lawyers filed applications for their clients. By the 1990s, approximately 5 per cent of the applicants were detained. In certain Member States today, we see that over 40 per cent of the applicants are legally represented before the Court. And of course, the fact that lawyers introduce applications means that the cases are as a rule well prepared and will concern all aspects of modern society.

H. Keller: I'd like to come back to one point made by *Christian Tomuschat*: the situation in Germany. Against the background of the comparatively good human rights situation in Germany, you have drawn a picture of the good guys and the bad guys among the Member States of the European Council. I would like to question two assumptions that probably are underlying this picture. The first assumption is: the better the human rights system in a country on the national level, the lower is the number of cases going to Strasbourg. At first glance this might be convincing. However, this is wrong. The Court's statistics tell us a different story. Even in the old Member States where we find a fairly good human rights system, the number of cases taken to Strasbourg is increasing. This is also true of countries like Germany, Austria or Switzerland. In these countries, we notice a shift in the character of cases. There, we do not find any classical human rights cases anymore but rather borderline cases or so-called fine tuning cases. The main issue is the balancing of interests. A good example for a fine tuning case in Germany is the *Caroline von Hannover* case and for Switzerland the *Stoll* case. What matters is the proportionality test and the balancing of interests. In such situations the crucial question is: what is the right role for the Court in these cases?

The second underlying assumption I challenge is: the lower the amount of applications going to Strasbourg, the better is the system of rights protection on the national level. There is neither a clear nor a simple linkage between those two factors. Take the example of Poland. Poland has no record of gross human rights violations; nonetheless, it is one of the best clients in Strasbourg, just because the Convention is extremely popular and the mistrust *vis-à-vis* the national judges is tremendous in Poland.

J.A. Frowein: A short remark concerning history. I think one should understand that the restrictive attitude which prevailed during the first ten years in the European Commission of Human Rights had something to do with the fear that if the confidence of Member States would be lost, this would really have the result that the whole system would fail. I don't pronounce a judgment on that. I was not a member of the Commission at that time, but when the Commission in the 1970s took a new approach, it was very clear that members of the Commission felt that either that system is going to work or it will remain, as *Christian Tomuschat* stated it, a sort of facade system. A very important role concerning that issue was played by the *Ireland v. United Kingdom* case. And therefore, I am of the opinion that interstate applications, although they are very few, fulfil an enormously important role. I fully underline what Judge *Villiger* has just said concerning the importance of the role of British lawyers, who had no internal system to turn to because no constitutional court existed and no real administrative court existed. But the role of British lawyers in this *Ireland v. United Kingdom* case was told to members of the Commission in a very personal manner. Somebody who later became a member of the Commission, *Sir Basil Hall*, said: we were all convinced that this Commission of continental lawyers would never be able to handle the facts of such a case. But before the Court, the United Kingdom government did not in any way contradict the fact-finding of the Commission. So this case played an enormous role for the authority of Commission and Court. I join *Erika de Wet* in her remarks concerning *Behrami and Saramati*. I would have thought the same as *Christian Tomuschat*, detention of personnel must be jurisdiction in the sense of Article 1. Unfortunately, we know now it is not, at least according to the Grand Chamber of the Court. *Acquis conventionnel*, this was the reason why members of Commission and Court went to the new accession countries and delivered reports. Unfortunately, the Council of Europe looked into these reports only to a very limited extent. There were political reasons for that. I may come back to that later.

J. Polakiewicz: I would like to continue where Professor *Frowein* has just stopped, with a theme also mentioned by Professor *Tomuschat*, the *acquis* of the Council of Europe. I think, in theory, everything was there to prepare these countries for accession. There was the political will and also in practice the required procedures were in place, at least to a certain extent. As Professor *Frowein* just recalled, before signing and ratifying the Convention, the Parliamentary Assembly looked at the national situation, looked in particular at the legal and judicial system of the candidate countries.

Former or actual members of the Commission or Court went to the candidate countries and prepared reports on their compliance with Convention standards. In its opinions that were a prerequisite for the Committee of Ministers' decision to accept any new Member State, the Parliamentary Assembly requested precise commitments, in fact long lists. The lists became longer almost with each accession, identifying to a certain extent also the Council of Europe *acquis* in the sense that they explicitly named the conventions that the country had to sign or ratify. They also listed the main structural reforms, such as reforms of the penitentiary system, the judicial system and so on. Then all this was followed up on the inter-governmental level as well as through cooperation and assistance activities. So there were actually procedures in place.

Why did they not completely deliver all the expected results? I think there are many reasons. One is obvious: there was not enough money for all the required assistance activities and structural reforms that were really needed. Another reason was a sort of perverse effect of the Assembly's monitoring of the commitments, which was in principle a good thing. But at the same time, the countries wanted to get off the list of countries under monitoring. They wanted to finish the monitoring exercise as soon as possible. So they ratified quickly these conventions, sometimes without doing their homework properly. And so many countries ratified the ECHR when they were still in transition, without having fully implemented all the reforms they had committed themselves to go through.

A second remark: although money is not the solution for everything, money is required for the Court's proper functioning, but not only. I think we need adequate financial means even more at national level.

What the whole system in Strasbourg is about and what is also stressed continually by the Court is subsidiarity. The normal and natural Judge of the Convention should be the national Judge. Human rights protection starts and ends at home in the sense that the national authorities should first look at what the Convention rights are, respect and protect them. Secondly, when a judgment has been given in Strasbourg, the execution, the implementation of the judgment must be done through national authorities.

To finish with a final information remark, there is now an interesting initiative in the Council of Europe, which will be voted by the Committee of Ministers during the next weeks. This is the creation of a human rights trust fund, an initiative by the Norwegian government, which will allocate money through the Council of Europe Development Bank for structural reforms in the Member States to ensure better compliance with the Court's judgments. I think this is an important initiative.

R. Grote: My first remark is of a technical nature. Professor *Tomuschat*, you compared the number of judges of the European Court to the 9 Supreme Court judges of the US. I ask myself whether this comparison is technically correct because it is the task not only of the Supreme Court judges but of all federal judges to enforce the Constitution of the United States and the Federal Bill of Rights. So it is perhaps more adequate to compare the number of ECtHR judges to the total number of Federal judges in the US. If you pursue the analogy further – particularly with regard to the Federal Appeal Courts – it is worth considering whether one of the possible reforms of the European system should not have as its object a stronger regionalisation of the ECtHR. Since this is a Court whose jurisdiction stretches from the Atlantic in the West to the Bering Strait in the East, it is perhaps not a bad idea to provide for a substantial measure of regionalization within the Court structure itself, by creating regional chambers or fully-fledged first-instance courts composed of judges with a specialized knowledge of the domestic legal system and the political and cultural context which is relevant to the application of the European Convention in the case at hand.

This brings me to my second remark. Our topic can be approached from two different angles, the European and the national perspective. Regardless of the number and the scope of the reforms which may (or may not) be implemented at the European level – e.g. the increase of the number of judges serving on the ECtHR, the reform of the Court's procedure, including the introduction of a European version of the *cer-*

tiorari procedure, etc. – the relationship between the ECtHR and the domestic courts remains of fundamental importance. Without functioning enforcement mechanisms at the national level the Convention will not achieve its main objective, i.e. effective protection of human rights. This raises the question whether there is any real prospect for the harmonization of the existing judicial mechanisms for the enforcement of human rights at the national level. As far as I can see, the existing national protection systems are still characterized by a high degree of diversity. There are some systems, like the Czech and the Slovak system, which allow their national courts to review the constitutionality of statutory acts and government measures not only in the light of the domestic fundamental rights bills, but also on the basis of the European Convention and other international human rights treaties to which the respective country is a party, whereas other systems, like the German system, do not allow the constitutional courts to apply the Convention rights or other international human rights as such in the review of fundamental rights applications brought under the relevant national rules on judicial review. Even worse, there are still systems in which individuals do not have direct access to their constitutional courts in cases concerning the alleged violation of their fundamental rights. In France, for example, the Constitutional Council still does not have the power to entertain individual constitutional complaints. Thus it seems that the task of harmonization to be achieved at the national level is indeed a monumental one.

F. Hoffmeister: I would like to thank Professor *Tomuschat* for his excellent overview and ask a short question on the remedies surveyed at the end. You did away with Protocol No. 14 by saying that the Russian obstruction is going to last for a long time. So we may not expect its early entry into force. While this is certainly true, my question would be: is there room for provisional application? Certainly, in the final clauses of Protocol No. 14 there is nothing about it. But can one not think that at least those States which have already ratified, so all Council of Europe members but Russia, could agree on a provisional application on those cases which do not concern Russia? Is that, let's say – an idea to be floated? Or would you argue that institutional revisions cannot be applied provisionally among certain parties only because there is a need for one valid procedural device for all cases?

K. Doehring: Only a short remark which I would like to make here. The situation in Strasbourg we are meeting now reminds me of the old and well-known story of the "Zauberlehrling". Please forgive me that I use a German word because German is usually prohibited here. But I have no other example to do that. This "Zauberlehrling" first activated the ghosts and then nobody knows how to stop them. That reminds me that the same question arose concerning the right of asylum. First, we sought to protect exceptionally prosecuted people and later on we had immigration. The situation is very similar here. So I think it would be better to consider the consequences before establishing principles of such a fundamental character. But we will see whether anybody has consequences to present here.

C. Tomuschat: May I say a few words. We are all experts here and accordingly there is no need for me to comment on everything that has been put forward. I would just respond to what *Karl Doehring* said. To me the balance sheet reached until now is wonderful. It's very good. And I see very few negative sides. We only have to keep the record, the good record. This is a challenge now after a good start of 50 years, of half a century. The European Convention has played a tremendous role in improving and raising the level of human rights civilization all over Europe. So I do not see the parallel with the right of asylum under the German constitution, which may have to be criticized to some extent, but here I think we have to reflect on how to maintain the advantages we have gleaned from the system.

I go back. *Frank Hoffmeister*. I think the only possible remedy would be to put Protocol No. 14 in operation with 46 ratifications, just discarding in a way the refusal of Russia by arguing that a single Judge can operate with regard to 46 States. This is not totally impossible. But of course, Protocol No. 14 would have to be revised. The relevant clause would have to be amended, but juridically it could be done. Normally, if you bring about constitutional reforms, institutional reforms, you need the approval of all current States parties. But here it may be that we would eventually have parallel to one another two different systems. One for Russia and the other one, the system proper, which would be somewhat more easygoing, for the other 46 States. It's a challenge and I don't know what the Russians would say about it, but it could be done.

Addressing what was said by Mr. *Grote*. I did not really compare the US Supreme Court and the European Court, I said, we may compare the numbers of now 47, maybe 94 in the future, to the nine judges of the Supreme Court, but I also said that such comparison is inappropriate because the European Court has much more to do. Therefore, that was just the start of my reasoning, and I added that this was a really inappropriate comparison.

Now, as far as *Helen Keller*'s observations are concerned. I do admit that I would have to look more carefully into the Polish cases. Is there some red thread in those cases? Do they reveal a systemic deficiency or not? Since there are so many cases, I am not quite sure. I guess that some people are here who could enlighten us on the Polish cases. The first enlightenment comes from my left-hand side, but maybe it should be made explicit for all other listeners.

And now coming to *Erika de Wet*. It's true that some States have had a long period of preparation, in particular France, not less than 30 years. They could adapt, they could observe how is the system going to work. And is it an unacceptable risk? But I am quite happy now that Russia, in spite of all the problems which have been entailed by the Russian accession, is indeed a State party to the European Convention and has just to comply with the relevant obligations. If Russia had been awarded also a period of 30 years from 1996 to 2026 before acceding to the European Convention, there would be no remedy suited to control what is going on in Russia. There are so many cases, I admit, that's a real challenge. But now we do have those remedies, which are more than political remedies. I am quite happy that the Court has to deal with the Russian cases and that we know that the Chechen cases and many other cases are pending. I do not envy the Court. And I really don't know what the Court can do in a true investment protection case like the *Yukos* case which embodies a new kind of challenge. How can the Court really cope with its duty of protection in such a difficult, complex case? I guess that, if I were a Judge, I would really tremble in being assigned the *Yukos* case.

And then the second, the *Bankovic* case. We will certainly be discussing the *Bankovic* as well as the *Behrami and Saramati* cases. I must confess that I am not absolutely impartial on those cases because I represented the Federal government in *Saramati*. And I must also confess that I am not unhappy with the result of the proceedings. Not only because of my special role. *Saramati* was really a special case because that person had been detained by a KFOR and not a Norwegian commander or anyone else acting under national authority. It was very clear, it was the structure of KFOR which was responsible. Since KFOR is not an individual State the Court rightly came to the conclusion that its responsibility could not be challenged before the European Court. Well, I admit that this is very much open for further discussion.

The Admissibility Stage: The Pros and Cons of a *Certiorari* Procedure for Individual Applications

Outline of Main Points

Rudolf Bernhardt

I. Facts and expectations

(1) In autumn 2007, for the first time in the history of the ECtHR, 100.000 individual applications were pending, 10.000 more than at the beginning of the year.

(2) It can be anticipated that both the number of applications and the number of pending cases will further increase.

(3) The unavoidable result must be that even in cases of grave human rights violations long delays and even a denial of justice are to be expected.

(4) The 14th Additional Protocol is still not in force. Even if it enters into force, the overall situation will remain precarious. The recommendations presented in the Report of the Group of Wise Persons cannot really help in the foreseeable future.

II. Pre-conditions for an effective reform

(5) Any effective reform requires far-reaching changes on several levels: in the Convention itself, and in the rules and the practice of the Court.

A considerable number of proposals with many details has been submitted, but they need not and cannot be repeated here.

(6) A reform should preserve as much as possible of the merits of the system, and it must also guarantee an effective and speedy procedure.

(7) The right of individual petition must remain the centre piece of the system.

(8) The author of this report is firmly convinced that only a radical reform is capable of producing an effective result.

III. Arguments against a discretionary admission procedure (or a *certiorari* procedure)

(9) It is alleged that an admission procedure which enables the Court to select, without giving reasons, the cases to be decided on the merits, is incompatible with European traditions and the proper function of a Court of Law.

(10) It is also argued that an admission procedure contradicts the requirements of an effective protection of human rights and the legitimate expectations of the potential victims.

IV. Arguments for a discretionary admission procedure and further aspects of a radical reform

(11) The existing practice, *inter alia* the declaration of the inadmissibility of applications which are "manifestly ill-founded", has already the consequence that more than 90 per cent of the applications are declared inadmissible. The reasons given for the inadmissibility remain often vague and unsatisfactory.

(12) A free selection within the discretion of the Court can and should take into account:

(a) The gravity and/or the unique character of the alleged human rights violation, and

(b) The general and systemic importance of the alleged violation.

Both considerations are of equal importance for an effective human rights protection in Europe.

(13) Only a reform of this kind could help to overcome the present difficult situation and prevent a future breakdown of the whole system.

(14) Cases of minor importance for the potential victim and without systemic implications must no longer be resolved on the international level.

(15) Practical solutions for the proposed reform can be found. The practices of some national courts, like the US Supreme Court, are not the right model for an international human rights court with 47 judges. A possible solution for the ECtHR could be (tentative proposals):

(a) Only a few changes to the Convention are necessary.

(b) A panel of the Court composed of the presidents and vice-presidents of the Court and the Sections would elaborate guidelines for the admission of cases.

(c) The Sections could to a certain extent concentrate on specific areas and decide which cases can and should be scrutinized on the merits.

V. Outlook

(16) In the view of the present author, a radical reform as proposed is necessary and possible. But much optimism is required to hope that such a reform will be accepted politically.

Transcript of the oral presentation of Rudolf Bernhardt

Dear colleagues, I should make a few preliminary remarks. According to the programme the speakers have only 20 minutes time for their presentation. Secondly, you have already seen a copy of my main points. I would like to add immediately that I start this presentation with point 7 of my outline. What is covered in the points 1 through 6 has either been said or will be said by others. Therefore, in view of my limited time contingent, I start with point 7.

The right of individual petition must remain the centre piece of the whole system of human rights protection in Europe. There is no other convincing possibility. Inter-state applications do not help. At present, there is one inter-state application pending: Georgia against Russia. There have been a few such applications in the past, but the whole system is based on the right of individual petition. And this must remain so. This does not mean that every individual application must be investigated in depth. But the starting point must remain the individual petition.

In point 8 of my outline, I give the essence of my report: I am firmly convinced that only a radical reform can help. If I am not mistaken, there are now three alternatives for the future development of the Strasbourg Court. The first is: wait and see what is happening without a far-reaching reform. This would mean that, in the near future, the system would either break down or the applicants will have to wait between five and ten years for their applications to be really scrutinized by the Court. If you look at the judgments of this year 2007, you very often see that the applications came to Strasbourg in the early years of this century, in 2000, 2001. If you look more closely to the facts, you see that very often the facts relate to the last decade of the last century. This is the present situation. Some internal improvements inside the Court and in its procedure are to be expected, but they will not really help to change the overall situation.

The second alternative is that only a limited reform takes place. Protocol No. 14 provides for such a reform. But this protocol probably will not come into force, even if there is still some hope that Russia will finally ratify. But even if Protocol No. 14 comes into force, the situation will probably only change to a very limited extent. Also the Report of the Group of Wise Persons contains no proposals which can be put into effect immediately. As far as the report contains concrete proposals, their realization could even have the consequence that the procedure becomes more difficult than it is at present, but there is no chance that such proposals will come into force in the near future.

So, I am convinced, and this is my point 8, that a radical reform is possible and would be able to preserve essential points of the present system.

I come now to point 9 of my outline. Let me make a few remarks concerning the headline above this point. I don't like the notion "*certiorari* procedure", because it gives the impression that one would like to follow entirely the American system. I think it is better to use another expression. I have called it "discretionary admission procedure". That means that the Court has the competence to declare admissible only those cases which deserve a deeper investigation and a reasoned decision on the merits. I know that this position is a minority position, but this should not exclude careful consideration of its merits.

In points 9 and 10 of the outline, I have summarized arguments against any discretionary admission procedure. I have seen many negative remarks on the *certiorari* procedure, also in the report of the Group of Wise Persons, which deals with this possibility only in a few sentences. Also the European tradition is often invoked in this context. At first one can doubt whether similar procedures cannot also be found for some national courts in Europe. But the whole system of the European protection of human rights is unique, and we should find the best solutions for this system. Tradition alone cannot give a decisive answer.

Another point mentioned concerns the legitimate expectations of the victim. Nobody can deny that a potential victim is disappointed if his/her application is rejected. But I see the dilemma as follows: the alternative is only that either an application is declared inadmissible without giving reasons, or the reasoning consists of a standard formula which does not really discuss the merits of the matter. This last solution seems to be predominant in recent practice. But is this really a solution which meets the expectations of the applicant? In the final analysis I do not think that the arguments of others summarized in points 9 and 10 of my outline are convincing.

Let me mention a few other negative aspects of the present situation. It would be extremely deplorable and unsatisfactory if the Court were to decide many cases without giving convincing reasons and guidelines for national judges and the legal community in general; I am afraid that this danger exists.

We have now the situation that more than 90 per cent of the applications are rejected or declared inadmissible in different manners. Letters are sent to the applicants by the registry mentioning shortcomings of the applications. Other decisions, which are sometimes published in the official reports of the Court, declare and describe on several pages that an application is manifestly ill-founded. Sometimes this is done by a majority against a strong minority in the Court. This is not the general rule, but it happens. The present practice is defended under the pressure of the great amount of applications and it is understandable that many different attempts are made to overcome the difficulties. As others have already said, the judges do their best, but the best is not good enough.

I now come to point 12 of my outline, which has a central place in my reasoning. The selection of cases for decisions on the merits should consider two alternatives: either the gravity of the alleged human rights violation, or the general and systemic importance of the alleged violation. I think that under the European system the Court cannot or should not reject cases in which grave human rights violations are alleged. This must remain one essential point in the selection and scrutiny of cases. One could add the cases where new and unique characteristics become visible, e.g. in environmental matters or in the field of data protection. The other alternative concerns the general and systemic importance of the alleged violation. This is the so-called constitutional aspect of the matter. Common European standards can and should be developed in many areas. If an individual case shows that this case is representative for defects in a certain national system, then the Court should take the case in order to investigate the matter also in general. This can have the consequence that a case which is in itself of minor importance gives the Court the possibility to discuss a certain systemic aspect and to give a reasoned decision on this systemic aspect.

Points 13 and 14 are partly repetitions, partly consequences of my proposals. I will not discuss them further.

I come now to point 15 of my outline. My first statement is that the practice of national courts is not the right model for an international human rights court with 47 judges. I assume that it will neither be possible to reduce the number of judges in the foreseeable future, nor will it be possible to have more than one Judge from every State. Both ideas have been put forward several times in the past, but I think that there is no chance that proposals of this kind may be realized. I would prefer the Inter-American system, which provides for only seven judges in the court, but I do not think that any of these proposals have real chances. There are proposals in the Group of Wise Persons, but I assume that it will remain for a long time the rule that all states which have ratified the European Convention on Human Rights have the right to nominate a Judge.

I have also said in my outline that my reform proposals require only a small number of changes in the text of the Convention. I would like to explain this in respect of one provision, namely Article 35 of the present Convention, concerning the admissibility criteria. In my view four conditions for admissibility should be preserved. The first is the six months period: applications are admissible only in the period of six months after the national decision is taken. I consider it also to be important that national remedies must at first be exhausted. This is a condition for the interplay of international and national judicial protection, also of the principle of subsidiarity. It is not correct to consider the exhaustion of local remedies primarily as a technical question. It is sometimes very difficult to establish and controversial whether the local remedies have been exhausted, whether there exist effective remedies, etc. But the exhaustion of local remedies must remain a centre piece of the whole system. This is my firm conviction. But if one would introduce a discretionary admission procedure, the Court would be able not to accept an application in which the exhaustion question is doubtful and when the case does not deserve further investigation. Two other conditions for the inadmissibility of an application do not need further comments: they concern the anonymity of an application, and the condition that the same matter has not already been submitted to another international institution.

I now come to two points which I have called tentative proposals. There exist undoubtedly some practical difficulties in connection with my proposals. If you have a discretionary admission procedure, the danger exists that five sections with chambers of seven judges are developing in different directions in respect of the admission of applications. My proposal is to have a panel which is responsible for developing more or less uniform practices of the different sections of the Court. This could be a panel with 11 persons, comprising the President of the Court, and the presidents and vice-presidents of the different sections.

Finally, I have formulated the proposal that the different sections of the Court should be able to concentrate on certain areas. For instance, one section would in first line be responsible for the right of freedom of expression, possibly combined with the freedom of association. By such a reform, it would be easier to develop coherent standards and to recognize necessary reforms.

I now come to my outlook. I am optimistic insofar as I think that the proposals just made could help to save the system and to develop it in a reasonable manner. But I am also pessimistic and doubtful that we can expect in the foreseeable future political solutions for the necessary reform of the present system.

Discussion Following the Presentation by Rudolf Bernhardt

R. Wolfrum: Thank you, Mr. *Bernhardt*, for your presentation. I share your concerns in respect of the system. And I see the wisdom of your proposal. Nevertheless, when you speak about, as you put it, discretionary admission procedure, I have my doubts. If you start with a purely, I add the word purely, discretionary admission procedure, can you really imagine that any case from a country which has a reliable human rights protection system would ever go to the Human Rights Court in Strasbourg? Or let's be more concrete: could you imagine that a case having been dismissed by the *Bundesverfassungsgericht* could be admitted under that procedure in Strasbourg? I have my doubts. This would raise the danger that this Court becomes a Court for certain States only, and this would definitely reduce the acceptability of the jurisprudence of that Court. Therefore my suggestion would be not to speak about the discretionary admission procedure, rather of a limited or restricted discretionary admission procedure and start with your points No. 12 a and b, and say that only in these cases, the Human Rights Court should have jurisdiction. In my view it is essential that cases come from all Member States. For example, the fair trial principle has also been violated by States such as Germany or Austria. And this was due to the length of the procedure or for other reasons. With the view to uphold or even strengthen the acceptability of the Court everything should be avoided to make the Court to be seen as a Court for particular States whose human rights record has been *a priori* considered as inferior and needs to be brought to a common human rights standard in existence before the membership was enlarged. Sure there are more cases pending from particular States such as Russia, for example. But these States should take some consolation by the fact that other States also do not have a perfect record.

A. Wittling-Vogel: I would like to make a few remarks. Mr. *Bernhardt*, I very much like your point 14. You say cases of minor importance and without systemic implications should or must no longer be resolved on the international level. I think this is exactly the reason for the new admissibility criterion in Protocol No. 14. It's absolutely clear that your proposed discretionary power goes further than the new Article 35 in Protocol No. 14. But I think if the Court wants to, it can go very far with this new admissibility criterion in the direction you propose. So maybe your case is not as hopeless as you said it was.

The second issue I want to raise is this: maybe I belong – as Mr. *Wildhaber* put it – to the friends of the applicants. We should not forget about the repetitive cases, because I think that if the Court had discretionary power, one of the effects would be that the Court would not decide all the repetitive cases. And this might not be the right way, at least in States where – as Professor *Tomuschat* said – the Court is nearly the only hope for many applicants.

The third point is: if we implemented a reform, a new protocol providing the Court with discretionary power, I am sure that, viewed on the political level, the budget of the Court would go down. The governments would say: what do you need so much money for? You are going to decide fewer cases. And that means that the Court would not be in a position to say: I am going to decide all the repetitive cases which I consider important to decide because the States do not comply with the judgments of principle. So that's another fear I have concerning this proposal.

J. Meyer-Ladewig: It was really interesting to listen to you, Mr. *Bernhardt*. This was one of the key problems of our reform discussions. And I can accept, and I fully agree with you that we need a drastic solution because other solutions won't help. But I think I am not quite so convinced as you and Mr. *Wildhaber* seem to be that your solution is inevitable. I still wonder whether other possibilities might be feasible. And I must confess I am also a friend of the applicants and the application. Mr. *Bernhardt*, in your point 7, you say the right of petition must remain the centre piece. That's certainly true. On the other hand, your proposal reminds me of the jurisprudence of the Court concerning the right to a Court under Article 6 I. When – in theory – there is a right to a Court, but the Court doesn't decide on the merits of a complaint, then we may have a violation of Article 6 I. And I wonder whether we don't have the same situation here. We say, following your proposal, there is the right to an application, but the Court does not decide in all cases, only in some. I think we must discuss two questions. The first question would be: is your proposal a solution that really helps? And the second question is: can we afford such a solution? Is it compatible

Discussion Following the Presentation by Rudolf Bernhardt

with the key elements of the Convention? And when, considering these questions, I look at your point 12, I wonder which cases you have in mind. What kind of cases will be accepted and decided upon and which not? I can imagine that Chechnya torture cases or violations of Article 2 will be considered as grave and will be accepted for decision. But what about all these repetitive cases where the reasonable time element is at stake, about 80 to 90 per cent of the judgments of the Court? I mean in particular complaints under Article 6 I and Article 5 III, sometimes also of Article 1 of the Protocol, e.g. where damages for expropriation have been paid late or a judgment of a national court has not been executed in time. Such cases often demonstrate a general and systematic violation of the Convention in a State and make clear that the human rights situation, the organisation of justice, is not satisfactory. When the Court under your proposal decides all these cases, this discussion is to no avail. So there must be a selection. And I wonder which cases fall outside the selection criteria. And in these cases which are not accepted, there I quite agree with Ms. *Wittling-Vogel*, there will be no protection at all. There are many applicants that can get protection of their individual rights only in Strasbourg, not by national institutions. And another main problem remains: who decides on the acceptance or rejection of a case? You said the committee or gremium will develop guidelines. Fine. But who decides whether a single case is accepted or not? It cannot be a single Judge. Perhaps it can be a committee or a chamber. Anyway – in the last resort, it will always be the Registry, I'm afraid. And we always had the idea that we don't want protection of human rights in the Court by civil servants, we want protection of human rights by judges. And that becomes more and more difficult. I know that the idea of a decision by a Judge in all cases is a bit theoretical already now. And unfortunately it becomes more and more difficult to achieve that aim. And when we see 47 judges and 580 members of the Registry, we must admit that this proportion is not so good. Mr. *Tomuschat* discussed the question of increasing the number of judges, he talked about doubling the judges. And when he said one has to reflect that, I quite agree. But possibly these judges must not be judges as we have now in Strasbourg, but as proposed by the wise persons a kind of judicial committee. You can name it as you want, but I think the idea that judges coming from the Convention States, young judges, but nevertheless with some experience, going to Strasbourg for a certain time or for a long time, being nominated, elected by the Court and forming a new filtering body, dealing with the cases that are or should be dealt with by the Chambers under the 14th Protocol, is worth while to consider. But if one takes that solution, of course, the workload of the Registry remains. But then there would be better possibilities to increase the number of the Registry staff. So, the main topics, to say it again, are: which cases, following your idea, shall not be accepted for decision by the Court? And the second question: are there not other possibilities to come to a solution?

A. Peters: Thank you, Professor *Bernhardt*, for the interesting presentation, which I think really goes to the heart of the theme of our conference. We have to ask ourselves the question: what is the proper role of the Court? We are contemplating a filtering mechanism in order to allow the Court to come back to its real function and get rid of the more marginal issues which block its activity now. I think that your proposal must be very seriously discussed. However, there are also important objections against a discretionary admissibility scheme. One frequent objection is that this would constitute a change of paradigm, because it abandons the principle that every applicant has an individual right of application. I am not convinced by this argument, because the Court's role is a dual one, both to secure objective justice (objective function), and to remedy individual cases of human rights violations (subjective function). This dual function is reflected in your point 12. If we introduce a discretionary scheme, this would signify a strengthening of the objective function and move the subjective function more to the background. The idea to allow for flexible shifting from one judicial function to the other is also what underlies the admissibility scheme of the German Constitutional Court. The relevant German statute uses the two criteria you propose in point 12. It is normally said that the German Constitutional Court does not have discretion: if the statutory conditions are fulfilled, it must take the case. But I think that the difference between this scheme and "real" discretion is more a theoretical than a practical one.

There are other objections which are probably more important. One is the danger that recalcitrant states will use the discretion as a pretext to formulate even more vehemently the reproach of a politization of the Court. This is a very serious objection and I do not know how to cope with it. Maybe we must revisit all other already suggested types of filter mechanisms, e.g. the establishment of a judicial body, not a body of civil servants, below the court. The Wise Persons' Report called this a "judicial committee".

Discussion Following the Presentation by Rudolf Bernhardt

J.A. Frowein: Thank you very much. My first question to Professor *Bernhardt* really joins Frau *Wittling-Vogel*. I would like to fully understand how you would compare what we have in Article 12 of the 14th Protocol, with the criterion "has not suffered a significant disadvantage unless respect for human rights requires an examination of the case". The "significant disadvantage" is really more or less the same as your substantial gravity of the alleged human rights violation. The general and systemic importance is underlying the respect for human rights as defined in the Convention. But I would like to have your view on that. If I remember things correctly, I was still in Strasbourg at the time when Article 37 was introduced into the Convention, Article 37 para. 1 c was seen at the time as a discretionary element for the Court because the Court could strike out any case at any stage of the proceedings for any other reason established by the Court if it is no longer justified to continue the examination of the application. This was seen by many as a possibility to reject cases without any real serious importance. On the other hand, this was clearly a very strange systematic place to put it because it was not in the admissibility criteria, it was a striking out thing and therefore misplaced. I don't know whether Mr. *Meyer-Ladewig* can enlighten us on how that really came about.

R. Bernhardt: First, I would like to say that I consider myself also to be a "friend of the applicants". But I am also a friend of the present system and of an effective international protection of human rights. And this general approach requires a selection of the applications which can or must be more closely scrutinized. The unavoidable consequence is that a great number of applications finally cannot be admitted.

I am also convinced that cases of less importance should be rejected without the necessity to give a reasoned decision. The present text of the Convention (Article 45) requires that in general reasons be given for all decisions. The practice is in my view not always in conformity with this requirement.

I wish to come back to the question whether my proposals may have the consequence that the Strasbourg Court would decide only cases coming from a certain group of states. I agree that this must be avoided, and it can be avoided. In the practice of the Court many cases concerning Western European States have been scrutinized, and violations of the Convention have often been found. Atrocities in police custody, deprivation of property without adequate compensation, violation of fair trial requirements can occur in nearly all States. Also systemic defects can and have been found in Western European States, e.g. the presence of representatives of the executive branch in court deliberations. All in all, I am convinced that the Court could practice a selection procedure which does not discriminate among the Member States. But if the prison conditions are unacceptable only in a small number of European States, it is clear that only these States pose problems in Strasbourg.

I now come to a few other questions raised in the present discussion.

Repetitive cases play an important role in the practice. In the past, the Committee of Ministers has as far as I know not only investigated whether a judgment of the Court has been executed in the individual case, but it has also asked which general or systemic consequences must be drawn. Now the Court has taken up this task, at least to a certain extent. I cannot discuss this question in further detail.

Can other solutions be found which may be less radical than my proposals and nevertheless have similar consequences? I can only refer to the following facts: even now more than 90 per cent of the applications are declared inadmissible or are not accepted for other reasons. The reasons given for the inadmissibility are in my opinion often not adequate or convincing; this is again understandable in view of the workload of the Court. Another fact: under the present system each year 10.000 and more applications are added to the number of cases pending at the end of the previous year. I am afraid that this number will further increase.

It is also argued that Protocol No. 14 may help in the future, and also Article 37 of the Convention (especially the second paragraph) can be used for rejecting more applications. I agree, but I am convinced that these provisions cannot adequately solve the problems, at least if they are applied in line with the underlying reasons.

M. Villiger: Thank you. Two concrete points in respect of your excellent presentation, President *Bernhardt*, and then a more general reflection. The point is well taken about the conflict potential between the different sections of the Court. The latter has indeed established a board which aims at preventing such conflicts. The board has different ways of doing so. It has procedures and it can ring alarm bells. These alarm bells ring before the sections deal with their cases. The section is told: "careful! Other sections have previously decided differently". The Court is still fine-tuning the system. At times, the board is issuing its warnings frequently, but in my view better too often than not enough. The second point is the quality of the judgments. They can never be drafted well enough. It is difficult to determine whether the judgments of the Court are activist or conservative. For every case which confirms one view, another case will prove the opposite. As regards the length of the judgments: the sections are called upon to prepare judgments which are more compact. The lengthiest judgments you will find in the Grand Chamber. Of the three last judgments of the Grand Chamber, let me mention two: *D.H. v. the Czech Republic,* concerning the situation of Czech Roma school children, and *Stoll v. Switzerland,* concerning the publication of a confidential diplomatic report, where Professor *Keller,* who is among us today, represented the applicant. These judgments are extensive and thoroughly reasoned precisely because they are important for all 46 and soon 47 Convention States. And in all fairness, even the old Court produced lengthy judgments. Now a more general remark: I am also a friend of the applicant and I think the right to individual application provides the democratic legitimacy of the Convention and the Court. We have 50.000 persons filing applications every year. Thus, 50.000 applicants express their confidence in the Court and in the Convention. They do so even if they know that some may have to wait for a long period of time until they obtain a judgment or a decision. 50.000 applications a year also imply that the Court will have to examine 50.000 real situations of the European society. If there is one thing one cannot accuse the Court of, it is that it does not know what is going on in real life. The Court as it stands today is certainly not a body that is in an ivory tower playing glass bead games. Of course this does not mean that we should not search for a solution. But we must see the positive side to all this. As President *Wildhaber* explained early on in the year, the problems facing the Court are problems of success, not of failure. We have to do something, but what? When President *Wildhaber* in 1998, soon after his election, was in Switzerland, he gave a speech proposing the introduction of *certiorari* proceedings and the abolition of the individual petition. This was in 1998. And still the Court is plodding on. We must find proposals; and we must find the time to do so. I note that last week the reflection group of the Steering Committee of the Council of Europe discussed various reform proposals, I saw that they had a list of over 90 ideas before them.

E. de Wet: The first of my two questions concerns the reasonable time criterion contained in Article 6 (1) ECHR. There is a perception that many if not most Member States prefer to risk a condemnation in Strasbourg for having violated the reasonable time criterion, rather than investing the necessary resources in reforming their judicial systems. Stated differently (and perhaps rather cynically), States regard it as more cost efficient to pay compensation to individuals that successfully claim a violation of the reasonable time criterion, than reforming their judicial system. This raises the question whether systemic solutions have been considered to solve the problems pertaining to the reasonable time criterion contained in Article 6 (1).

The second question pertains to the suggestion that the ECtHR should in future only concentrate on grave and systematic human rights violations. Which criteria would be applied during the admissibility phase in order to determine whether one is dealing with a grave and systematic violation? Would, for example, the systematic infringement of civil liberties (e.g. Article 5(4), Article 6(1) or Article 8(1) ECHR) resulting from anti-terror legislation adopted after 9/11/2001 qualify as grave and systematic human rights violations? Or would only (widespread) violations of absolute rights such as the prohibition of torture qualify as grave and/ or systematic?

S. Oeter: The question which is puzzling me is a more practical question. I understand that one of the decisive bottlenecks in the system is the capacity of the staff, of the Registry. That's why we have this discussion on doubling the number of members of the staff in order to cope with the number of applications adequately. And what is puzzling me now is: to what degree does the idea of a discretionary procedure on taking cases really cope with that problem. I assume that every case even in a discretionary system has to be dealt with in substance, a member of the staff has to look into it, has to write a report in order to enable the single Judge or the committee to take a learned decision. So to what degree is there really a rationalizing effect concerning that point? I am sure there is a rationalizing effect concerning the other limited resource, which is the working capacity of the 47 judges. There it might really help them to concentrate on the important cases and to be speedier. But on the other part, I don't see the big advantage, or at least it is a question to what degree it helps. And is there an alternative really to aggrandizing the staff with the ensuing problem of creating a monster Court. If you want to avoid that – is there an alternative to cutting it again into two pieces like the old Commission/Court system, if you want to have institutions which might handle the caseload adequately.

T. Marauhn: Following our discussions so far, it is my impression that we are all presenting guesses, guesses about the credibility of the system. Unfortunately, we don't have sufficient empirical knowledge at our hands as far as the perception of the Court by complainants or actors involved is concerned. While we all agree that the credibility of the Court must be preserved, we do not know how to achieve this objective. Judge *Villiger* referred to the number of applications as evidence of the Court's credibility. Professor *Bernhardt*, on the other hand, pointed out that by not giving reasons for some decisions, even though procedural ones, the Court will probably be derived of some of its credibility. This raises the question of what is essential for the credibility of the European human rights system. I think we haven't answered that question. But we must find an appropriate answer to it because otherwise we will fail to get proper perspectives on a reform of the system. Let me add one facet to our debate: so far we have not mentioned the debate about the reform of the Federal Constitutional Court Act in Germany, which illustrates some of the problems with *certiorari* procedures both at a practical and at a theoretical level. The debate doesn't discount those procedures. But I think we should look more closely into why the reform of the German Federal Constitutional Court Act failed. And we should draw our lessons from that experience.

L. Wildhaber: Mr. *Bernhardt*, I very much liked the presentation that you gave and also that you insisted that the system must be stopped from being overloaded and overworked and must be made to work again. There is simply no alternative to the Court.

To Judge *Villiger*, I would say I am somewhat puzzled. *Certiorari* is technically speaking a writ, an order of the Superior Court to a lower Court to submit the file of the case to the higher Court so that it can decide on it. Now the ECtHR has plenty of cases where there is no decision of a lower court, be it because the national remedies are inadequate or because there is a length of proceedings problem. So I would be somewhat disappointed to learn that I have advocated, without reservations and without these additional explanations, that there should be a writ of *certiorari*. As I said, the problems begin to be complex.

I suppose we all believe that we are friends of the applicants. It is therefore helpful to discuss how the system can meaningfully survive and how those applicants that really are in need of help and whose human rights violations are grave are treated with priority by the Court. I'll finish with one story of mine being last year in the fall in Moscow at Radio Moscow. I was interviewed by a journalist and then outsiders could call in. Someone said that he had written to the Court more than three years ago and had not got as much as an acknowledgement of receipt. I was defensive, but he was adamant and insisted, so that I encouraged him to write a letter to me, and I would see what I could do. That was the end of the programme. All lines broke down, everybody wanted to relate that they were in the same situation. If we allow that to go on, are we still friends of the applicants?

P. Mahoney: I should like to try and give a practical answer to the question raised by *Stefan Oeter*. Beforehand, however, I would like to make a few introductory remarks.

The right of unimpeded access to Strasbourg has tremendous symbolic value. "Europe" has a bad reputation with the ordinary citizen at the moment. It represents grey men in grey suits in Brussels who decide how much malt you can have in your beer or how much humidity you can have in your sausages. It is hermetic to the ordinary person. The ECHR, in contrast, provides a mechanism that is accessible to everyone. And once in a while, the citizen wins a famous victory against his or her government.

On the other hand, the willingness of national supreme and constitutional courts to apply and even bow down to the Strasbourg case law is based on the quality of the judgments in the few meritorious cases deemed to raise a genuine human rights issue. As soon as that quality disappears, the vital link of trust between Strasbourg and the national systems will likewise disappear. It would therefore be an error to focus exclusively on the right of access of every individual to the Court in Strasbourg. The treatment of the mass of applications that are lodged cannot be given priority to the extent of undermining the examination of the meritorious cases. It comes down to a question of balance.

Thirdly, it is evident that the present structure for processing cases in Strasbourg does not correspond to the reality. It is not working. If something is not done, the system will simply seize up and break down. I agree that the starting point for looking for solutions is to ask the basic question: "what is the mission of the ECtHR in Strasbourg? Why do we have a ECtHR? What do you want it to do?" If you look at the myriad of circumstances in everyday life that can give rise to an allegation of a violation of one of the rights or freedoms guaranteed by the Convention, you can see that it is simply not conceivable to expect that this Court in Strasbourg will be in a position to give an individual examination to every complaint that is received and to provide individualized relief, even in the event of a violation being found to exist. This is simply not possible in material terms. Hence the need to have a different, more limited conception of the role of the Court.

Discussion Following the Presentation by Rudolf Bernhardt

In this connection, it makes little or no sense for the 47 judges on the Court, the top constitutional judges in Europe, to spend a substantial part of their time personally examining the thousands and thousands of unmeritorious applications lodged. That is why the idea of a separate filtering mechanism, operated perhaps by junior judges, has been proposed. A simple system whereby such junior judges can take a decision after briefly examining the files is needed. If the filtering judges are in their turn to be required to spend hours examining the file, the whole point of a simplified, streamlined separate filtering system is lost.

I personally believe that the best criterion for filtering out unmeritorious applications was the one put forward in the (2001) report of the so-called Evaluation Group, which was the first of the recent spate of reports into the functioning of the Convention system (*Luzius Wildhaber* being one of the three members of this Evaluation Group). One of the proposals made in that report was to amend the Convention so as to empower the Court to decline to examine in detail applications raising no substantial human rights issue under the Convention. That admittedly is a criterion which contains a discretionary element.

In answer to *Stefan Oeter*'s query whether a discretionary filtering criterion would in practice rationalize or reduce the overall level of work in Strasbourg, I would readily agree that an initial filtering process which is to deal with an enormous volume of applications, especially if it is to be operated by inferior judges, must be based on simple, clear and easily applied rules. This is necessary to ensure consistency across the board. With applications coming in from many different countries – Bulgarian cases, Russian cases, Romanian cases, German cases – it would not be acceptable to have different kinds of discretion being applied in relation to cases of similar content, especially if the judges are "junior". Furthermore, if the filter has to exercise discretion in the light of the particular circumstances in each case, the basic aims of a simple filtering system are not met. As I see it, the discretionary element could only serve a meaningful purpose at a higher level of jurisdiction – that is to say, doubtful cases should always be handed on up the line by the junior filtering judges to the elected judges. This was the proposal the Court itself made at one stage: that the initial filtering mechanism would be responsible for sifting out the *manifestly* inadmissible cases, but not for generating case law on admissibility conditions and not for exercising discretion. The arguable cases, including the arguably admissible cases and in particular those where it is not clear whether the application is to be classified as the kind of case which does not raise a substantial human rights issue, would go up the line. When there has been accumulated a sufficient accretion of instances of a reasoned exercise of discretion in a particular direction, in a particular category of case, then the Court's case law would have established a principle that could be applied as a bright-line rule in a similar way across the board for all the different junior judges.

I do not think that I am revealing any secrets of the way the Registry works by saying that it is organized as a kind of factory with production lines to process the mass of committee cases through standardized procedures and standardized solutions, set out in handbooks that are translated into all the languages for all the different language divisions. I always used to explain this approach as being a bit like the food-production procedures imposed by McDonald's so as to ensure the same quality, the same taste and the same service in every McDonald's wherever you go in the world. Likewise, the Registry is concerned to make sure that all the different language divisions dealing with hundreds of comparable cases a day, as they do, apply comparable procedures and comparable solutions. Similarly, it is perfectly conceivable to have a discretionary filtering criterion (interpreted by elected judges) combined with a very simple "mechanized" separate filtering mechanism (operated by junior judges).

A filtering system can be described as a sort of tap or safety valve to control the flow of cases to the Court. There is a real, and pressing, need for such a mechanism, which I do not believe to be contrary to the principle of the right of individual petition. In my opinion, it is far from wise to structure the system such that the number of cases that have to be examined on the facts and on the merits can go on increasing exponentially every year. There must necessarily exist a saturation level for the number of cases that 47 judges can adjudicate on properly in one year. There is a ceiling of probably 200 or 300, maybe 400, cases maximum per year in which the Court can be expected to deliver a proper, reasoned judgment. This being so, the Court needs a tap to be able to limit the flow to that maximum level, which is where the discretionary element proposed by Judge *Bernhardt* would come in.

C. Tomuschat: Very few observations because most of what should be said has already been said. I think we all agree that the Strasbourg system should not break down. We also know that justice is a scarce resource. This is also a truism. Not everyone can bring his or her case to international review. And therefore, light cases should be thrown out. On the other hand, review of individual cases should be maintained as a matter of principle. The Court should not withdraw to a high and dry fortress where it would only rule on principles. Such a reform would be a bad mistake. Of course, to rely on the repetitive character of certain factual patterns is not a suitable recipe. There can indeed be atrocious patterns of repetitiveness: for instance, if police forces go out to kill people every night. Such evil practices can never be discarded as cases where the law stands firm and does not need any further corroboration. In the past, some light cases were dealt with by the Court. I recall in particular the Austrian case of *Adolf* (A 49, 26 March 1982) where the presumption of innocence was an issue. Somebody had thrown a bunch of keys at another person, apparently causing some light injury. When the case was terminated without any pronouncement on the merits, the tribunal concerned stated in its decision that the complainant was guilty but that his fault was insignificant. It cannot be denied that the case involved a matter of principle, but as to its factual dimension it was indeed insignificant.

My conclusion is that we need indeed a filtering system. But we should avoid the concept of 'discretion' in that regard. Decisions should be based on reliable criteria. Nonetheless, one should not believe that you can take decisions without ever being challenged because allegedly what you did was not really rational or objective. Unavoidably, there will always be some attack if you sort out, if you throw out certain cases. That difficulty should not prevent us from promoting the reform process. I agree that not every case where possibly a violation has occurred can be examined in great detail.

R. Bernhardt: I am grateful for those who have approved some of my points, and I am also grateful for those who are in opposition. I cannot deal now with all points and questions raised.

There seems to be an overall agreement that the starting point should be the investigation and the judgment on individual cases. There is no alternative to that. But it is also correct to state that individual cases can often have repercussions for many other cases and areas.

In respect of some proposals concerning a new filtering system, I have mainly the following difficulties. Under the present system and also under Protocol No. 14, there are two grounds for the inadmissibility of applications: applications may be manifestly ill-founded, and the second point is the non-exhaustion of local remedies. In these two fields, there have often been so many extremely difficult legal questions that I have doubts whether these problems can be solved by other persons than the judges of the Court. Admissibility questions and the merits of a case are often so closely connected, that also in this respect only the usual members of the Court should decide.

Another practical point: the staff in the Registry now comprises more than 500 persons. They are able to deal possibly with 80 to 90 per cent of all applications, but 10.000 and more cases remain without a final decision. In order to deal with these still pending applications and all incoming applications in a reasonable time, several hundred more persons employed in the Registry could be necessary. This again would aggravate the difficulties to coordinate the work of a great number of persons and bodies.

Finally, I would like to come back to the necessity that the judgments of the Court and the reasons given in these judgments must be adequate and convincing. The Strasbourg system has undoubtedly very much improved the international protection of human rights in Europe. One essential reason was that the great majority of all judgments have been convincing. It would have helped if the national judges were more familiar with the Strasbourg case law, if translations of the judgments were available, etc. In this respect, many improvements are possible and required. But it remains essential that the judgments and their reasons remain convincing.

On the other side, if you consider the cases decided by the Strasbourg Court more closely, you will find a considerable number of cases which hardly required an international control in addition to the protection.

The Interaction Between National Protection of Human Rights and the ECtHR

Jochen Abr. Frowein

1. The jurisprudence of the Convention organs has had a historic influence on the legal systems of Western European Member States. These States have accepted judicial review of legislation through the Convention organs and many have introduced judicial review of legislation on the basis of constitutional or similar instruments. The case law of the Convention organs has contributed to strengthening judicial review of administrative decisions where it did not or not fully exist before. The guarantees of an open democratic process, in particular concerning freedom of expression have been strengthened or introduced into legal systems where they did not have the same rank before. The principle of proportionality for State interference with individual rights has been introduced in all Member States. In that respect Convention law and European Community law have been of equal importance. One may even come to the conclusion that Convention law has influenced the legal systems of Member States in a more dramatic way than has European Union law. However, this is not always fully noticed, not even by lawyers.

2. For some of the transition countries the same development has started after 1990. However, specific difficulties have arisen in some countries, in particular in Russia. There is no doubt that the transformation of legal systems in several of the transition countries has been highly influenced by the ECHR. This is evident if one looks at the constitutions of the former communist countries. However, it is also clear that in some of these countries special problems arise. To take Russia as an example the number of cases, the apparent impossibility to improve the internal situation as far as courts and prisons are concerned show a real difficulty. One does not need to address such issues as Chechnya to come to that conclusion.

3. In the present situation the ECtHR can be compared to a sinking steamer. The day can be calculated when the system becomes inoperative. One may discuss when it would become really inoperative. But it seems clear that where the number of cases not dealt with outnumbers the others in an extreme manner one could no longer speak of an operating ECtHR.

4. States have always been ambivalent as to their support for the Strasbourg system. Compared with the EU Strasbourg has not been given sufficient means to develop in a comparable way as the European Court of Justice. This refers to budget, staff, means for translation etc. It is to a certain extent ununderstandable that we get European Court of Justice case law concerning agricultural matters or subsidy issues immediately in the language of the States concerned but that this is not true for Strasbourg. One could argue that it would be much more important for the Strasbourg judgments to have them immediately in the language of the State concerned because they frequently affect all the citizens. The Luxembourg judgments frequently concern only rather limited groups of corporations or individuals.

The non-ratification of Protocol No. 14 by one of the Member States is in my mind an issue which could give rise to legal proceedings. A Member State which has seriously violated Article 3 of the Statute of the Council of Europe can be suspended or even excluded on the basis of Article 8 of the Statute. If one analyses Article 3 it is telling that the obligation to and I quote "collaborate sincerely and effectively in the realization of the aim of the Council as specified in Chapter I" is laid down as an obligation. Chapter I Article 1 contains the obligation to pursue the aims of the Council of Europe by agreements and in the maintenance and further realization of human rights and fundamental freedoms. The question can well be asked whether the non-ratification of a protocol which has the aim to improve the dramatic situation for the ECtHR is not a breach of these obligations. To my knowledge no justification for this action has been given at all.

I am of course fully aware that my remarks are only theoretical and there is no possibility to act on this basis. However, what should be clear is that a State which is not willing to cooperate in the improvement of the situation for the ECtHR should not remain a member of the system.

5. Statistics show that the internal protection of Convention rights is of high influence for the number of cases declared admissible by the ECtHR. In fact, the impressive statistics offered by *Stephen Greer* show that there is a clear relationship between the internal system protecting

fundamental rights and the number of cases declared admissible in Strasbourg. The influence of the British Human Rights Act is, as far as I know, not yet clearly visible from statistics but will certainly show the same pattern. Therefore, it is of great importance that States improve their internal systems for the protection of human rights.

6. To cope with the high number of applications a filtering mechanism in the judicial systems of Member States should be introduced. I am aware of the filtering mechanism proposed by the group of wise persons. It may be that such a procedure could help although I have my doubts. I would rather opt for a filtering mechanism to be decided by Member States on the basis of their authority to lay down the principles of exhaustion of domestic remedies.

7. This mechanism would consist of special chambers on the Supreme Court level of Member States for dealing with Convention cases. Before an application could be lodged to the ECtHR an appeal to this chamber would be necessary as part of the exhaustion of domestic remedies. This procedure would prolong internal proceedings. However, this seems unavoidable if one tries to reduce applications to the ECtHR. Of course, this would not be necessary in States where one has already a similar system. In Germany it would not be necessary if the Federal Constitutional Court would become serious in applying Convention case law. At the moment the situation is not really clear.

8. A special effort should be made by Member States to inform courts about the case law of the ECtHR. This information is frequently lacking. The Council of Europe could also become active in this field. Translations should be soon available in the language of the country concerned. This should at least be true for important cases with consequences for the entire legal system.

9. Member States must become serious in avoiding repetitions where the ECtHR has found a violation. In particular in matters where pilot judgments have been rendered it is necessary to adopt legislation or other measures to avoid repetitions.

Member States should not question judgments of the ECtHR after they have become final. However, the ECtHR must also be careful not to overstep its jurisdiction. There are a few examples where it can be argued that the Court has gone too far. It is in particular a bad example for the authority of the ECtHR when a Chamber overlooks that its judgment does not become binding before three months have elapsed.

On the other hand the German Federal Constitutional Court has unfortunately given a very bad example when it introduced the notion of sovereignty to argue that under certain circumstances judgments by the ECtHR could contradict constitutional rules in Germany. The Court has not clarified under what conditions that could be the case. It seems to be a completely theoretical argument which was unnecessary under the circumstances. However, such precedents weaken the Convention system at a time when it is crucial to strengthen it.

10. Conclusion

Unless Member States really become willing to strengthen the Strasbourg system it may be seen after some years as an example of fundamental rights case law in Western Europe which could not be transferred to the new Europe. This would be very unfortunate. For somebody who has worked with the Strasbourg system during 20 years at a time when the first important development of case law took place the present situation may be called sad.

Of course, similar problems existed already when the number of applications to a then part-time body, the European Commission of Human Rights, grew in the second half of the 1980s and in the 1990s. I remember very well our internal discussions when the big wave of Italian length-cases arrived at the Commission. I argued at the time that only with creating a special channel for dealing with these cases we would be able to avoid being sunk by the sheer numbers. To a certain extent we managed to create such a channel. It was not fully satisfactory but it certainly helped to overcome the difficulties.

I very much hope that Member States but also those involved in Strasbourg will find ways and means to overcome the difficulties.

Let me also mention the relationship to the European Union at the end of my remarks. I find the way the Charter of Human Rights is now being sold as a great step forward in the European Union system somewhat strange. The applicability of the Charter will be very limited indeed. An opt-out system has been accepted. One should hope that the role of the ECtHR will be strengthened within the Council of Europe and the Strasbourg system will remain the important centre for the development and guarantee of the European human rights system.

Discussion Following the Presentation by Jochen Abr. Frowein

K. Doehring: My question is: what is the binding force of the decisions about which we should inform the Courts and so on. That is a question of *res iudicata* and one must take into account that principally the decisions are working only *inter partes*. Moreover, the Court, and that's important for me, could change its own view and a Constitutional Court can do so also, and what's then the existing law? So even by repetition, there might occur a certain change of the Court's opinion for a similar case in a new situation and the case was lost. So I doubt whether the information about existing law could stabilize the legal situation.

H. Keller: I want to comment on three points of your talk against the background of my research project on the reception of the Convention in Europe: on the issue of translations, the exhaustion of local remedies, and finally on the reception that must take place before a case is tried.

First, I absolutely agree that translations of judgments are crucial for the success of the reception. However, in our research project, we found that, particularly in the new Eastern European Member States of the EU, Strasbourg judgments are translated only in so far as they concern one of these countries. This is true, for example, in Poland, where all "Polish" judgments are translated – involving issues of "lengthy procedure" over and over again. No other cases coming from other countries – regardless of how important they are – are translated. Focusing only on national judgments for the translation is a limiting and misleading strategy and finally a real shortcoming in the diffusion of information.

My second point is about the exhaustion of local remedies. I think this is in general an underestimated question in the interaction between the Convention and the national system. I remind you of the Polish case *Szott-Medyńska* where the question was if Polish applicants had to go first to the Polish Constitutional Court in order to fulfil the requirements of Article 35 ECHR. It is a hotly debated question in Poland. This interaction between national human rights protection and the European level is cost-intensive (in terms of time, money and intellectual efforts). This problem has to be examined more closely in the future, in particular against the background of the Court's heavy docket.

Third, in our research project we examined how national parliaments are dealing with the Convention. The reception process has to start much earlier than before the courts. In many countries there is no established institutionalized process for the systematic control of draft bills for their compatibility with the Convention. In this area, much has yet to be done.

A. von Bogdandy: I would like to stress the importance of the interaction between the national protection of human rights as well as the European Convention and the European Court. I truly share your idea that we need a stronger focus on the national system. However, I would challenge the underlying idea that we have had so far; namely, that the protection of human rights is above all a matter for the courts. The point I want to make is that, if we want to get to grips with the situation, we need to develop administrative law to implement human rights. I think we need that and we need it at the internal level. Of course, courts are important, but courts cannot manage the task on their own, there needs to be a more systematic implementation which depends on agencies – on bureaucracies. Such a bureaucracy is actually underway: the European Union Agency for Fundamental Rights. It is not a national, but as a part of the EU machinery it is an internal agency. This agency is currently in search of a mission; its agenda has still to be adopted. This requires a decision by the European Council of Ministers. Consequently, the point I want to make is that in addition to what has been said, there should be a systemic link between what the ECtHR is doing and the mission of the agency. In my understanding, the mission of that agency is to scrutinize very closely what is happening once the Court has pointed at a systemically deficient situation in a country in order to then use the full panoply of EU instruments and to come to terms with that situation. This is in particular promising because the instruments of the European Union, if the agency works closely with the Commission, are very strong and in any case much stronger than those of the Council of Europe. As a result, my idea is that we don't need to alter the Court itself, but make use of the existing mechanism at hand; that is the agency. It's only necessary to give the agency the mission – the guidelines – to look into systematically deficient situations in Member States because – and that is very important – the agency is only one element in a broader network of human or fundamental rights institutions. Under the respective regulation every Member State has to set up national institutions which monitor the human rights situation in the country. These are full elements in the domestic system, and as such, very powerful. So my point is that, in order to improve the situation, there must be a systemic link between the ECtHR and the European Union Agency for Fundamental Rights, which then empowers the Court's decisions with the full panoply of European Union instruments and domestic instruments within the network of fundamental rights institutions.

R. Müller: You said on the one hand that Member States should not question the Court's judgments, but on the other hand, you admitted that the Court sometimes goes too far. Don't you think that the Karlsruhe warning – don't touch our sovereignty, (whatever that means) – can be a useful threat as it is maybe already as to the Luxemburg court although it remained theoretical until now?

A. Peters: I would also like to follow up on the *Görgülü* judgment. I fully agree that the tone and the use of the word sovereignty were probably superfluous and even detrimental. But overall, the judgment was ambivalent and also had, astonishingly, a quite positive effect on the German judiciary. It triggered a much more intense and more frequent discussion of the European Convention by German judges, more quotations and real analysis of the Convention and case law. This is so because the regular courts now know that if they do not take the Convention "duly into account", to use the expression of the Constitutional Court, this will give rise to a constitutional complaint. This is a very welcome development. Moreover, a recent chamber decision of the German Constitutional Court extended the constitutional obligation to take international law into due account beyond the European Convention. That chamber decision held that decisions of the International Court of Justice must be taken into account. In the concrete case, the German criminal courts had not taken properly into account the Vienna Convention on Consular Relations and the respective ICJ case law. The constitutional complaint which had argued this was declared meritorious. This seems to be a very positive spill-over effect of the *Görgülü* decision.

J. Polakiewicz: First of all, you will not be surprised that I can agree with practically everything that you said. I will just make a couple of comments. I think what will be crucial, indeed, will be the relation with the European Union in the future in this area. I think it is very significant that the Treaty of Lisbon, which was just signed last week, will, once ratified by the Member States, provide a legal basis for accession by the European Union to the ECHR. Moreover, there is even a commitment for the Union to accede. This will finally bring the systems of Strasbourg and Luxemburg together. This will be of importance, I think not so much because the EU does not protect human rights, I think the EU has an excellent record in this area, but from the symbolic point of view. It will be important that Strasbourg is not seen as something alien or separate from the EU legal system but as part of it.

The point made by Professor *Frowein*, the Convention as the reference point for the whole of Europe, was made precisely in the Memorandum of Understanding, which the Council of Europe and the European Union concluded in May this year. It was a long negotiation and it was not easy to convince everyone, both in Strasbourg and Brussels, but the point was finally made.

So with both the Memorandum of Understanding and the Treaty of Lisbon, we have a good perspective for the future. The Council often needs the political power of the European Union to make States implement its standards. I have, on the other hand, some hesitations about the Agency's role as described by Professor *von Bogdandy*. I think the idea is very appealing. The Agency does not have a very clear mandate, it is still searching its place among the existing human rights institutions in Europe. But there are certain limitations to its potential role in ensuring the implementation of the Court's judgments.

First of all, so far at least, the Agency has no competence in the third pillar. The European Convention's case law is about, to at least more than 50 per cent, criminal law and its application, in particular the fair trial guarantees. The Agency's remit may change once the Treaty of Lisbon will be in force, but for the time being at least, criminal law is outside the Agency's remit.

Secondly, the Agency's basic functions are data collection and analysis, not monitoring of compliance. However, one should not forget that in the Council of Europe there is also the Commissioner for Human Rights, who is in fact more and more turned to as an institution to help implement the Court's judgments. He is working closely with the network of national human rights institutions. The idea, both expressed in the Wise Persons' Report and various Committee of Ministers' declarations, is that he should have a stronger role regarding the implementation of structural reforms in the Member States. So I think the Commissioner can be a central figure in this area, too.

E. de Wet: Professor *Frowein* suggested the introduction of a special chamber dealing with ECHR cases at the highest courts of Member States (see point no. 7 on his list), as a mechanism for lightening the caseload of the ECtHR. On the one hand, this solution may bring significant relief in States with well-functioning legal systems. On the other hand, the question arises whether such a mechanism would yield the same results in Member States with weak or badly organized judicial systems. Unless the functioning of the relevant judicial system as a whole is improved, the State in question may still face a large number of complaints in Strasbourg due to a violation of the reasonable time criterion in Article 6(1) and/ or the absence of an effective remedy on the domestic level.

As far as increased knowledge of the ECHR is concerned, countries like the Netherlands and Belgium have come a long way since ratification. In both countries most practicing lawyers are nowadays familiar with the ECHR, it has become important in the political discourse and generally receives a good press. However, although this increase in knowledge and visibility has strengthened human rights protection in both countries, it cannot in and of itself prevent ECHR violations. Ever so often critical questions posed by members of Parliament or advisory bodies such as the Council of State are brushed off by government officials or even ignored. Effective domestic implementation remains a complicated issue. Although improved knowledge of the ECHR constitutes an important element in or even a prerequisite for this process. One should not underestimate the ability of those exercising public power to adapt to changed circumstances and find new ways of evading obligations under the ECHR – despite enhanced knowledge of the ECHR within the legal community and society in general.

J.A. Frowein: I'll make a few remarks concerning these first interventions. I agree that of course judgments by the Court are binding only between the parties. But that doesn't mean that they should not be taken into account where they concern wider issues. And in fact, as the Court has started with the pilot procedure, which we will discuss tomorrow, the obligation of 46 clearly goes beyond the specific case. Translation – I think this is a very important point. Constitutional Courts as being required under the exhaustion of domestic remedies system; I think this is fully correct, wherever there is a possibility. This may take a little time with countries like Poland. But this should not be underestimated. With regard to Parliament; I fully agree, the necessity to discuss issues of the Convention when legislation is being drafted is frequently underused in Convention countries. I have difficulties to fully accept the Agency idea brought forward by *Armin von Bogdandy*. First of all, I think, as others have stated, the Agency in many areas has no jurisdiction whatsoever. And this would of course be the first question to be asked, whether there is any jurisdiction under European Union law. Even if there is jurisdiction the Agency is set up in a way which cannot really enforce anything and I doubt whether it is correct to say that the European Union system which exists for violations of European Union law could be combined with the Agency's jurisdiction. So far I must say I cannot really see that. Concerning the interpretation of the *Görgülü* decision by the Federal Constitutional Court and the comparison with Maastricht, I of course agree that something can be said for the Court's line in Maastricht and others. I have much more difficulty coming to the same conclusion with *Görgülü* because there was no issue whatsoever of interfering with German constitutional law. However, I think Frau *Peters* made that point, although only indirectly and maybe without wishing to express it fully, the criticism of *Görgülü* has led to the ICJ case. The Court in Karlsruhe all of a sudden noticed what it had done and wanted to redress to a certain extent in the ICJ case. Yes, EU/Strasbourg, Mr. *Polakiewicz*, I fully agree that it is of course an important step with the ratification of the new treaty that accession will become possible. I admit that I have always been a bit sceptical about what accession can really improve. But I'll not go into that in detail now at this moment. I think what should be really avoided is – and there I see a great difficulty in the political discussion these days – that the European Union with the Charter system somewhat tries to occupy the ground which the ECHR for very good reasons has occupied since 1950. I think there is a very clear tendency for that. Frau *de Wet* asked the question whether the special chamber system could work for instance in the transition countries. I think it could for the following reason: the problem of information of lawyers is a very real problem. And as soon as you would have a specialized chamber, where you could really expect people to know the case law of the ECtHR, it would make a lot of sense to force people to go there. In fact, if you analyze what has happened in some of the member countries, the specialization of specific courts in Convention matters has helped very greatly. The Swiss Federal Tribunal has started very early on without having a very clear mandate for that, really going into Convention law, telling the cantonal courts, the other courts that they must respect Convention law. I have always argued that the Swiss were much better than the

Germans. So I make it very clear: I am not at all convinced that the Germans always have the good way.

J. Meyer-Ladewig: I would like to say again a few words concerning the German Constitutional Court, the *Görgülü* judgment. I fully agree with you, Mr. *Frowein*, and you, Ms. *Peters*, who said this judgment has positive effects. When you have a look at the case law of the Constitutional Court, you see that there is really a development. The Court in Karlsruhe goes more and more into the case law of the Strasbourg Court which in former times was a rather rare situation. That is a positive element, but there are certainly negative elements, as mentioned by Professor *Frowein*. And I would quite agree and say: this reasoning in the *Görgülü* decision of the Constitutional Court is deplorable. That is so because sometimes our national judges feel that they are left alone. These clauses as mentioned by the Karlsruhe Court are so general that in a given case, judges really wonder: are we bound or are we not bound by this Strasbourg judgment? And the most deplorable thing is that these reasons give States which do not like the Court supervision weapons to evade it. And the reasoning was not necessary. All these sentences are *obiter*. And so the question is: why did the Constitutional Court consider it necessary to bring these reasons? And I sometimes wonder whether it might have been a reaction to certain judgments of the Strasbourg Court, in particular the *Caroline von Hannover* judgment and the *Görgülü* judgment. Perhaps people feel – and I must personally say with regard to the *Görgülü* judgment I feel the same – that the Strasbourg Court did go too far, overstepped a certain borderline and should have been more wise, more prudent. In the *Görgülü* judgment, the Strasbourg Court said very clearly: the result of this judgment is that the father must have access to his child. And that was not very wise to say because in all these cases and in particular in family matters, the time element is important. After so many years have passed the situation now may very well be totally different. And so it would have been much better if the Court had said: the result is that the German courts have to reconsider this case and take into account the ECtHR's reasons and reflect the question.

A. Seibert-Fohr: I would like to come back to your suggestion to enhance domestic procedures which, to my mind, is a very valid proposition and most probably the right way to go forward. You mentioned the idea of special chambers on the Supreme Court level and I am wondering whether we could give some incentive within the Conventional system in order to enhance this kind of domestic implementation. My idea is to combine Professor *Bernhardt*'s proposal of a discretionary admission procedure or *certiorari* review with your proposition to enhance domestic application. It goes this way: once there has been review by a domestic chamber, the ECtHR could limit itself to cases of high gravity and to those of general and systematic importance. This would work like a system of carrots and sticks. The carrot is the limitation of judicial review in case States provide for judicial review on the basis of the Convention by State highest courts. If this is not the case the ECtHR, as a matter of sticks, should retain its uncompromised jurisdiction. Do you think that this could be an idea for the future? There is already some indication in Protocol No. 14 which points into this direction. However, I think that the provisions are not strong enough, yet.

A. Weber: I have one question. I think my point is very much along the lines of *Erika [de Wet]*'s and Frau *Seibert-Fohr*'s interventions; it relates to your proposal under point 7: the filtering mechanism consisting of a special chamber of the Supreme Courts. I have to express some doubts in this regard, not concerning the new Member States, but one "old" State, my country of origin, namely France. What are the Supreme Courts in France? You know the Constitutional Council is not perceived as being a Supreme Court because it cannot be seized by the individuals. Therefore, we have two Supreme Courts: the Court of Cassation on the one hand, the Council of State on the other hand. How do you imagine such a filtering mechanism in France? As you certainly know, these two courts had a different approach concerning the application of the European Convention in France. The Court of Cassation started already – well, it was quite late – in 1975 to apply the Convention, while the Council of State waited until 1989 to control the conformity of national norms with the European Convention. So what I see here is a risk of double standards, not only between the different Member States, but within one country. Considering the different approaches of the two courts, I think there is a risk to have such a mechanism.

F. Hoffmeister: I would like to make a few comments on the protection of human rights on the EU level and its relationship to the Strasbourg system. As regards cooperation of courts we have reached a phase where the European Court of Justice nowadays fully follows the guidance of Strasbourg and cites jurisprudence *in extenso*. Recently, Judge

Rosas has written an article entitled: "With a little help from my friends", where he makes the point that since the beginning of the 1990s there is a clear tendency of full cooperation. And I assume that the accession of the EU to the Convention will only strengthen this tendency, in particular given that the EU Charter on Fundamental Rights itself regards the standards of the Convention as the minimum and as an inspiration and not as something to be taken aside. As to the interesting idea of Professor *von Bogdandy* on cooperation at the administrative level, one can make two observations: the EU has been quite strong in the past in addressing systematic issues in accession countries. So, in the yearly progress reports of the Commission, the jurisprudence of the Strasbourg Court *vis-à-vis* the candidate countries was an important reference point when telling these countries: can you please address this or that human rights problem as a matter of EU *acquis*? For example, the length of proceedings in several of the 10 new Member States was a big point, where improvements were asked as a matter of *acquis communautaire*. Currently, *vis-à-vis* Turkey, there are a lot of issues like rights of minorities, religious associations, foundations and so on. And again, Strasbourg's jurisprudence is the reference point. In other words, one can argue that systematic issues are addressed by the EU's political institutions in order to help implementation of the Court's judgments. Administrative cooperation is less obvious with respect to situations in the Member States since an important question of competence arises. Below the threshold of Articles 6 and 7 EU, the Commission has limited possibilities to address systematic human rights issues on Member States' levels. Already with respect to the EC Regulation establishing the Human Rights Agency, there was a big fight about the appropriate legal basis: how far can one go on the basis of Article 308 EC? The compromise formula was to say: well, domestic situations can be covered if there is a link to Community law and its application in the Member States. Against this background, it would be interesting to hear your ideas how exactly there should be a link between the EU and the Strasbourg system given the EU's limited powers in the field. But definitely the idea could be explored.

M. Villiger: I have two matters. The first is on the provisional application of Protocol No. 14. This is possible according to the Vienna Convention on the Law of Treaties and has been applied in practice with certain protocols to the Convention. Protocol No. 1, for instance, has not been ratified by Switzerland, Protocol No. 9, which is now obsolete, allowed in respect of certain States for the applicants to go before the Court and others not. As regards Protocol No. 14, many commentators are adamant that this is an integral instrument, where you cannot divide up the Convention procedures among States. In fact, there are various points in Protocol No. 14 where the Court can hardly act differently according to whether a State has ratified it or not. For instance, we cannot say that one group of judges will have a single nine year period of office, and another group two six year periods. It would also not be possible to have the single Judge for applications against certain States and not against others. To some extent the Court has in its own way provisionally applied Protocol No. 14. For instance, the non-judicial rapporteur, a Registry member, is responsible today for cases brought before a Committee, which amount to over 90 per cent of the Court's output. The other matter concerns the comments by Mr. *Meyer-Ladewig*. You mentioned two points; one was that the Court was far away from reality in the case of *Görgülü v. Germany*. I am not so sure. It was the Naumburg Court of Appeal which didn't grant the visiting rights. Previously, the District Court, the Amtsgericht, actually ordered the visiting rights – and did so three times. How can one say the Court was far away from reality if it supported the District Court, which was closest to the applicant? Could one not say that it was the Court of Appeal which was actually distant? The other point: you said that because of the Strasbourg case law, the decision in *Görgülü* took too long. Of course, the Strasbourg Court must always critically examine the length of its own proceedings. But was it not also the Court of Appeal which took a long time to decide – *inter alia* by refusing twice to comply with the Federal Constitutional Court's judgment? It took them so long that at the end the Court of Appeal judges had criminal proceedings instituted against them!

A. Wittling-Vogel: I happen to be the national liaison officer for the Fundamental Rights Agency in Vienna and that's why I might be able to provide some information. Until now, there have been no plans for country monitoring. What the Agency does at the moment and will do during the next year or so is that it collects data on certain questions, which can also, of course, reveal shortcomings in certain countries. But this will not be carried out with the aim of monitoring a certain country as far as a certain problem is concerned; rather, the aim is to give an overview concerning several or even all countries as far as a certain question is concerned. For instance, they plan to collect information on children's rights. They were asked by the European Parliament to do this work. And the Council will soon produce a draft of the multiannual framework which is foreseen in the regulation.

That means that there will be a framework for five years with several thematic areas. But the framework will include only the thematic areas and not what the Agency is going to do within those areas. This is the state of play at the moment.

K. Schmalenbach: I would like to comment on points 6 and 7 of Professor *Frowein*'s paper and draw your attention to the practical problems in connection with the introduction of a special "Convention chamber" into the national judicial systems. I assume it is widely known that the European Convention on Human Rights is part of the Austrian Constitution, and that it is applied by the Austrian Constitutional Court, always with a view to Strasbourg jurisprudence. However, the Constitutional Court is not competent to review the judgments of the two other Austrian courts of last instance, i.e. the Supreme Court in matters of private and criminal law and the Administrative Court in matters of administrative law. In other words, in case a high court decision deviates from Strasbourg jurisprudence, the Austrian legal system does not provide for a constitutional complaint in order to safeguard a homogenous application of the ECHR. Right now, there is a vivid political discussion in Austria on the introduction of a "Urteilsverfassungsbeschwerde" (constitutional complaint against judicial decisions) into the constitutional system so as to guarantee a uniform human rights jurisprudence – so far with no success at all, due to the heavy protest of the Austrian high courts. They regard a reform of that sort as an unjustified reprehension. What is the consequence of the unwillingness to reform the Austrian court system? Well, Austria will continue to "outsource" human rights-based complaints against national judgments to Strasbourg and will thus continue to contribute to Strasbourg's workload.

C. Westerdiek: I have been very impressed by today's presentations, by the concerns and proposals expressed in the presentations and the contributions. I can only vividly recommend to do something of a filtering nature, whether at the Court level – I have my doubts whether an appropriate solution can be found – or better at the national level. And I would take on and continue on the remark by *Mark Villiger*, who has reported that, following recommendations of the Working Party on Working Methods of the Court, a group composed of judges and Registry staff, some of the ideas of Protocol No. 14 have already been implemented. I refer to the filtering process at the Registry level in respect of Committee cases. Several Registry rapporteur teams deal with all new incoming mails, filter Committee and Chamber work, and prepare the Committee for consideration, by now still the three-member Committee. This new approach has shown at the Registry level that it is important to separate the filtering and Committee work and the processing of meritorious cases. At the judges' level, no such separation is currently possible: judges are sitting in Grand Chamber cases and in the weekly Chamber sessions, which include large numbers of repetitive cases, they have to prepare Chamber cases as Judge rapporteurs in giving instructions or looking through new drafts presented to them. At the same time, they get on a two-weekly basis a bunch of notes prepared for the examination of Committee cases. Three judges per Committee have to comment within a short time-limit on some 100–150 Committee cases or even more. In this situation, what is called the "bottleneck" might at some stage no longer be with the Registry. The Registry staff can be increased, though to a limited extent per year (in addition to the normal turnover in the staff of the Registry, 75 new staff members can be integrated if the necessary budget increase is agreed). However, how long will judges still be able to cope with the increasing workload, if nothing changes? The high quality of judgments and thereby the authority of the ECtHR must be ensured for the future. In conclusion, I would reaffirm my personal preference to have cases with systematic violations resolved at the national level.

J.A. Frowein: I try to be rather brief. I think Frau *Westerdiek*'s last intervention has made it very clear how important it is to try to find additional means on the national level. And I must admit, I found Frau *Seibert-Fohr*'s idea to combine that with the *certiorari* idea very interesting and possibly quite fruitful. I am not at all convinced by the interventions concerning France and Austria. I think they rather prove the contrary. France as well as Austria would be very well advised to come to grips with these internal problems. I have argued that in Austria so many times and I have written on that. This all goes back to *Hans Kelsen*, who was of the opinion that the Constitutional Court, the Administrative Court and the Austrian Supreme Court must be on the same level. And he was very strong, as we all know, he forced his ideas through. But it is ridiculous that Austria is still stuck with that problem today. If you had a concentrated control in a Supreme Court chamber or senate or Constitutional Court chamber or senate, this could help really a lot. Herr *Hoffmeister*'s reference to the improvements brought about for the new Member States on the basis of European Union pressure combined with *acquis conventionnel* of course is something very relevant, but it does not help in the same way for old Member States as we know. The Agency has been discussed and Frau *Wittling-Vogel* has explained again how limited the possibilities of this Agency are. The provisional application of Protocol No. 14; Judge *Villiger* has told us what can be done in practice, but a real provisional application is excluded by law. I'll be able to explain that, I do not do it at this moment. *Görgülü*; I think both are right. And I have said so in my intervention if you recall it. On the one hand, the Federal Constitutional Court is really to be blamed for the slogan concerning sovereignty and all that ridiculous stuff. On the other hand, the ECtHR was to be blamed because they said something on the basis of facts known to them which dated back about 2 years. And in a family access issue, you cannot base your unconditional access rule on facts which you do not know. That I have written and I remain convinced that that is correct. Of course, in the case it didn't play any role. It didn't play any role because the facts had not materially changed.

Now, thank you very much for all the criticism and remarks. I think we have to think about it again and will hear very important interventions tomorrow. Let's hope that what I called a sad lookback to where one had been involved for quite some time, is not finally as sad as that and there is still a bright prospect for the future. Let's hope so.

Pilot Judgments in Cases of Structural or Systemic Problems on the National Level

Luzius Wildhaber

It is well known that one of the biggest problems facing the Convention system is how to deal with large numbers of well-founded applications deriving from structural problems existing in the Contracting States, the so-called repetitive cases. Many of these situations are found in the newer members of the Council of Europe, but the best known category of repetitive case concerns the problem of excessive length of proceedings in some of the older Contracting States; already in the 1990s large numbers of Italian length of proceedings cases were being processed and in due course it was found that the problem existed in at least half of the Member States. This state of affairs was encouraged by the Audit Court of Italy that commented that it would be cheaper to let all the cases go to Strasbourg rather than to reform the Italian judicial system. It can be said incidentally that the problem does not exist in those countries that have effective national remedies and otherwise it does exist. It was not until the *Bottazzi* judgment in 1999[18] that the Court noted that there had been an accumulation of identical breaches which were sufficiently numerous to amount not merely to isolated incidents, but to reflect a continuing situation that had not yet been remedied and in respect of which litigants had no domestic remedy. The Court did not at this stage itself seek to identify any general measures to correct this situation or indeed even call upon the Italian government to take general measures. The *Kudla v. Poland* judgment came only later when the Court began to see that there must be a national remedy under Articles 6 and 13 to take care of the problem on the domestic level. The general problem was recognized as coming within the responsibility of the Committee of Ministers.

---

[18] *Bottazzi v. Italy* [GC], no. 34884/97, ECHR 1999-V – (28.7.99).

Following the entry into force of Protocol No. 11 in 1998 other categories of structural situations began to emerge: thus the non-execution of final judicial decisions is a chronic problem in practically all countries of the former Soviet Union, except the Baltic States, and also e.g. in Romania and Bosnia-Herzegovina. Other issues include severe overcrowding in detention facilities again in several countries, delayed or inadequate compensation for expropriation, different problems with remand proceedings, and State Security Court cases in Turkey.

In the years following 1998, as the Court's general case-load continued to grow, it became clear that further reform was necessary and that any such reform would need to address the problem of repetitive cases. The solution offered by the resulting Protocol (No. 14) was the new three-judge Committee competence. However, the Court had called for the inclusion in the Convention of what has become known as a pilot judgment procedure.

The Steering Committee rejected this proposal, mainly because they were wary of the complications that might ensue from creating a legal obligation to introduce retroactive measures. But the Committee affirmed quite clearly that in their view it would be possible for the Court to introduce such a procedure under the existing terms of the Convention[19]. Moreover, as part of the package of measures accompanying Protocol No. 14 the Committee of Ministers adopted Resolution (2004) 3 on judgments revealing an underlying systemic problem in which it invited the Court "to identify, in its judgments finding a violation of the Convention, what it considers to be an underlying system problem and the source of this problem, in particular when it is likely to give rise to numerous applications, so as to assist States in finding the appropriate solution and the Committee of Ministers in supervising the execution of judgments".

The Court needed no further encouragement. In June 2004 it adopted the *Broniowski* judgment[20] concerning a compensation scheme for Polish citizens displaced after World War II from the regions east of the river Bug. Although the expression "pilot judgment" does not actually appear in the text of the judgment, *Broniowski* is clearly a new type of judgment, whose main elements are:

---

[19] See paragraphs 20 and 21 of the Interim Activity Report of 26 November 2003 (CDDH (2003) 026 Addendum I Final).

[20] *Broniowski v. Poland* [GC], no. 31443/96, ECHR 2004-V – (22.6.04).

(a) a finding by the Grand Chamber that the facts of the case disclose the existence, within the relevant legal order, of a shortcoming as a consequence of which a whole class of individuals have been or are still denied their Convention rights;

(b) a conclusion that these deficiencies in national law and practice may give rise to numerous subsequent well-founded applications. At the time of the Court's examination of the case, there were 251 pending Bug River cases and a potential for 80.000 new cases (please interpret these numbers and understand that the pilot judgment did not actually reduce very much the workload of the Court, but it did prevent the workload from exploding further);

(c) a recognition that general measures are called for and guidance as to the form which such general measures may take;

(d) an indication that such measures should have retroactive effect;

(e) a decision to adjourn consideration of all pending applications deriving from the same cause;

(f) the use of the operative part of the judgment to reinforce the obligation to take legal and administrative measures;

(g) reserving the Article 41 issue;

(h) information to the Committee of Ministers of the Court's approach in the case and the periodic provision to the Committee of Ministers, the Parliamentary Assembly and the Council of Europe's Human Rights Commissioner of the further developments in the case.

The Court stressed that the measures to be taken must be such as to remedy the systemic defect underlying the Court's finding of a violation so as not to overburden the Convention system with large numbers of applications.

The *Broniowski* judgment was followed a year later by a strike-out judgment[21] in the same case, which expressly considered the implications of the pilot judgment procedure. Here again the Court recalled the growing threat to the Convention system and to the Court's ability to handle its ever increasing caseload that resulted from large numbers of repetitive cases deriving from, among other things, the same structural or systemic problem. It further indicated that the pilot-judgment procedure was primarily designed to assist the Contracting States in

---

[21] *Broniowski v. Poland* (friendly settlement) [GC], no. 31443/96, ECHR 2005-IX – (28.9.05).

fulfilling their role in the Convention system by resolving such problems at national level.

The terms of the settlement concluded by the parties expressly stated they were intended to take into account "not only the interests of the individual applicant ... and the prejudice sustained by him ..., but also the interests and prejudice of complainants in similar applications"; and stressed "the obligation of the Polish government under Article 46 of the Convention, in executing the principal judgment, to take not only individual measures of redress in respect of Mr. Broniowski but also general measures covering other Bug River claimants".

Where are we with the follow-up to *Bug River* applications?

The new Polish compensation scheme was put to the test following the adoption of the friendly-settlement strike-out judgment. Fifty cases were chosen for this purpose. The applicants in all those cases were advised by the Court to avail themselves of the new compensation remedy, although it was stressed that it would be for the Court in the final analysis to determine whether the remedy was effective. The applicants were also advised of the procedure to be followed at domestic level for claiming compensation. All these applicants applied for and obtained compensation, although in many cases they were dissatisfied with the amount received.

Two test cases were subsequently identified with a view to determining whether in the light of the compensation scheme introduced by Poland, the issues raised by Bug River applicants can be considered resolved. The Court should decide on the matter shortly.

Since *Broniowski* in a number of cases the Court has sought to follow a broadly similar approach which has however disclosed divergences of practice.

In *Lukenda v. Slovenia*[22], a Chamber judgment from the third Section, in October 2005 concerning length of proceedings, the Chamber recalled the persistent backlog in the Slovenian courts in general, noting that there were some 500 Slovenian length of proceedings cases pending before it. The Court was therefore confronted with a systemic problem that had resulted from inadequate legislation and inefficiency in the administration of justice. To prevent future violations of the right to a trial within a reasonable time, the Chamber encouraged the respondent State to either amend the existing range of legal remedies or add new remedies so as to secure genuinely effective redress for violations of that

---

[22] *Lukenda v. Slovenia*, no. 23032/02 (Sect. 3), ECHR 2005-X – (6.10.05).

right. The Chamber did not, however, take upon itself to adjourn the pending cases. In a partly dissenting opinion Judge *Zagrebelsky* expressed the view among other things that the Chamber should have relinquished jurisdiction in favour of the Grand Chamber as the proper forum for identifying the existence of a systemic problem and drawing the necessary consequences there from. He also distinguished between the obligation to introduce a remedy and the obligation to take all the necessary measures to ensure that the right to judicial proceedings within a reasonable time was respected; the latter he felt could only be properly enforced and supervised by the Committee of Ministers.

In *Xenides-Arestis v. Turkey*[23] of December 2005 a Chamber of the Court was faced with one of the so-called post-*Loizidou* cases involving the denial of access to property in Northern Cyprus. The Chamber held that the respondent State must introduce a remedy, which secured genuinely effective redress not only for the applicant but also in respect of all similar applications pending before the Court. Such a remedy was to be available within three months from the date on which the judgment was delivered and the redress should occur three months thereafter. These directions were included in the operative part of the judgment. That three month period expired on 22 March. The Chamber reserved the question of the application of Article 41. Pending the implementation of the relevant general measures, consideration of all applications deriving from the same general cause (around 1.400) was adjourned.

In Scordino v. Italy[24] (March 2006), a case referred to the Grand Chamber, the Court found a double systemic problem, firstly in relation to the failure to afford adequate compensation following expropriation and secondly in the operation of the Pinto law. In respect of the failure to afford adequate compensation following expropriation, the Court indicated that the respondent State should remove every obstacle to the award of compensation bearing a reasonable relation to the value of the expropriated property. As regards the Pinto law awards, the Court invited the respondent State to take all measures necessary to ensure that the domestic decisions were not only in conformity with the Court's case law but were also executed within six months of being deposited with the registry. These indications did not appear in the operative pro-

---

[23] *Xenides-Arestis v. Turkey*, no. 46347/99 (Sect. 3) (Eng) – (22.12.05).

[24] *Scordino v. Italy* (no. 1) [GC], no. 36813/97 – (29.3.06).

visions of the judgment and no mention was made of adjourning consideration of similar pending cases.

In the *Hutten-Czapska v. Poland*[25] case the Chamber had held that the principles established in the *Broniowski* case applied, the more so as the operation of the rent-control scheme in issue might potentially affect even a larger number of individuals – some 100.000 landlords and some 600.000 to 900.000 tenants. Here too the facts revealed the existence of an underlying systemic problem, which was connected with a serious shortcoming in the domestic legal order. That shortcoming consisted in the malfunctioning of Polish housing legislation in that it imposed on individual landlords restrictions on increases in rent for their dwellings, making it impossible for them to receive rent reasonably commensurate with the general costs of property maintenance.

The government successfully requested referral of the case to the Grand Chamber, contesting the application of the pilot-judgment procedure.

However, the Grand Chamber agreed with the Chamber's conclusion that the case was suitable for the application of the pilot-judgment procedure as established in the *Broniowski* judgments.

As regards the general measures to be applied in order to put an end to the systemic violation identified in that case, the Grand Chamber considered that the respondent State had above all, through appropriate legal and/or other measures, to secure in its domestic legal order a mechanism maintaining a fair balance between the interests of landlords, including their entitlement to derive profit from their property, and the general interest of the community – including the availability of sufficient accommodation for the less well-off – in accordance with the principles of the protection of property rights under the Convention.

These directions were included in the operative part of the judgment. It should be noted that there are relatively few similar applications pending in Strasbourg (around 18), so that the effect sought is primarily preventive, given the very large number of potential applicants. There is an analogous Czech case, *Vomočil*, which has already been communicated to the Czech government.

It can be seen from these cases that the Court is feeling its way as regards recourse to the pilot judgment procedure. There appear to be several variants and this recognizes the flexibility needed to accommodate the range of different situations with which the Court is confronted. Thus in some cases the Court will go further in specifying the type of

---

[25] Hutten-Czapska v. Poland [GC], no. 35014/97, – (19.6.06).

general measures required, sometimes include its recommendation as to general measures in the operative part, sometimes adjourn consideration of similar applications.

The feature common to these cases is the attempt to address a problem affecting large numbers of persons through a judgment in an individual case, whether this is expressly acknowledged or not. This is in one sense merely a logical extension of the obligation to take general measures following the finding of a violation, with the added requirement that such measures must be retroactive so as to offer redress in particular to all those with applications already pending before the Court. Once again this recognises that some situations cannot be dealt with effectively purely by the judicial processing of individual cases. Some commentators have seen in this development a conscious move towards a constitutional court-type jurisdiction; others consider that it is more a pragmatic reaction to the realities of the problems facing the Court.

As acting President of the Court I would have stopped here. As past President, I shall take you one step further to the level of execution. What chance does a pilot judgment have of being fully implemented and executed? The *Broniowski* judgment was particularly well-suited to the pilot-judgment kind of adjudicative approach; the Polish Constitutional Court and the Polish government were receptive to that approach; so in essence there was not much resistance. That is likely to be different in other categories of cases. Much will therefore depend on the positive attitude of the respondent governments. And in the Committee of Ministers, which should act forcefully and coherently, governments might be committed to less than forceful execution standards, at least where their own interests are – or are believed to be – at stake. Even if the Committee of Ministers were replaced by a more independent supervisory body, ultimately the execution of judgments is in the hands of the national governments and the Committee of Ministers, acting together in good faith, provided always that good faith can be taken for granted.

Discussion Following the Presentation by Luzius Wildhaber

M. Villiger: Thank you very much for your excellent presentation, *Luzius* [*Wildhaber*], whereby you also elaborated on the profile of pilot judgments. I think pilot judgments have been misunderstood in some audits and also by well-wishers to the Convention pronouncing themselves on reform proposals. It would be wonderful if pilot judgments could resolve thousands of applications in one go, for example applications concerning the length of proceedings. But they can't. Pilot proceedings presuppose very particular circumstances, as a rule a legislative norm which leads to thousands of cases all with the same parameters. Take for instance the case of *Vomočil and others v. the Czech Republic* currently before the Court. These cases concern Czech rent legislation which potentially may affect thousands of proprietors (and, incidentally, also tenants). These cases are similar to *Broniowski v. Poland*, but there are certain differences.

J. Polakiewicz: I also was very impressed by this comprehensive presentation. I have mainly two questions and the first one is related to the binding force of these judgments. In particular, you made the good point that there are different cases and the pilot judgment character was not explicitly included in all of them in the operative part of the judgment. Parallel cases were then not always adjourned or even declared inadmissible. But I think in some cases this was actually done. In these cases at least, if the pilot judgments have a direct effect on other applications that have been introduced but which were of course not part of the proceedings which led to the pilot judgment, how can this be explained in terms of *res iudicata*? Is there not a sort of binding effect? The pilot judgment has had consequences on other pending applications. How can you reconcile this with the idea that normally the binding force only operates between the parties to the case?

My second question: you explained very well in the introduction that there are many areas where there are systemic or structural problems in Member States. However, there are very few cases where pilot judgments were actually used. The term was explicitly used in only two or three judgments and even if you add the other ones, which use similar language but without using the term, you come up with four or five judgments. Why not more? Is it because of reluctance by the States parties or because of uncertainty about the consequences? Can you say anything about this?

My last point is simply to add one bit of information. Apart from Resolution (2004) 3, there is also Recommendation (2004) 6 on the improvement of domestic remedies where the Committee of Ministers addressed the issue of pilot judgments. It is interesting to note that in the appendix to this recommendation, the Committee of Ministers states that one should not have a solution "one size fits all". They stress there can be cases where you have general new remedies or *ad hoc* remedies, but they add that it would not be necessary nor appropriate to create new remedies following every case in which a Court judgment has identified a structural problem. In certain circumstances it would in fact be unfair to the applicant to bear the further burden of having once again to exhaust domestic remedies, which, moreover, would not be in place until the adoption of legislative changes. You must be aware that in some cases it may be quite difficult for applicants to go back home and to go through domestic procedures once again. So it is not always the best solution.

A. Peters: Thank you for the very lucid presentation. I have two questions following up what Dr. *Polakiewicz* just asked. The first question: is it by accident that the few pilot judgments (except the atypical one, *Scordino v. Italy*, on the length of proceedings) have been issued only against new Member States? Does this mean that systemic problems exist only in the new Eastern Member States or are there other reasons for not issuing pilot judgments against the "older" Member States? My second question: how do you relate the pilot judgments to the proposals to issue judgments of principle or to equip judgments with an *erga omnes* effect, which would obviously require a treaty reform? Do you see the pilot procedure as an evolution in that direction?

C. Tomuschat: Well, my question is the same as that just put by Mr. *Polakiewicz*. What is the status of parallel applications? And if someone of the applicants insists that his or her case should be heard: have those applications become obsolete or moot? On what criteria can one rely in not adjudicating them? Is there any specific basis in the Convention which may justify leaving them formally unresolved?

F. Hoffmeister: That was also my question. What is the legal basis for striking off where a pilot judgment has been rendered and an appropriate remedy has been instituted? Could it be Article 37 (1) (c) of the Convention? And just a remark which could be of interest relating to the cases concerning the Northern part of Cyprus (*Xenides-Arestis*) that you have mentioned. Before the European Court of Justice a preliminary reference is currently pending which concerns also a case of a Greek Cypriot refugee (*Apostolides v. Orams*). He has obtained a judgment to demolish a villa by a British couple on his property in the Northern part of Cyprus and is now seeking recognition in the United Kingdom under the Brussels I regulation. In that case the question comes up: would such automatic recognition not have an effect on the domestic remedy established in the Northern part of Cyprus following the pilot judgments of your Court? And could there be an international public policy reason for the UK courts to refuse that? So that could be another case of interaction between those two high courts.

J.A. Frowein: Concerning the pilot judgment procedure, I agree to a certain extent with President *Wildhaber*. It's a new name for an issue which has been an old one before the Convention organs. Let me take the *Dudgeon* case where we found that the homosexuality legislation in Northern Ireland interferes with the right to privacy. It was of course clear that this interfered with rights of many others living in Northern Ireland. And it was also clear that there was an obligation under Article 53 of the Convention to amend the legislation. As long as the legislation existed, Mr. *Dudgeon* was of course clearly affected. Now the matter is a bit different I accept for the *Bug River* cases. You could say: as soon as the one person Mr. X has received compensation, there was no longer an obligation to amend the legislation, and I have written on that long before the pilot judgment idea came up, that if you combine Article 53 and Article 1 of the Convention, now Article 46 and Article 1 of the Convention, in cases where you can read from the judgment that a violation in absolutely parallel cases will be the consequence of a judgment, the State is under an obligation to amend legislation. And I think it's no difficulty concerning the *res iudicata* issue because the State is the party in the proceedings. And proceedings may have the consequence that the State has obligations not only to a given request from a particular applicant but also to repeat legislation. Since President *Wildhaber* has mentioned the *Xenides-Arestis* case, I must say this was an unfortunate start of the procedure. Why was it an unfortunate start? Because the Chamber said: you have to do it within three months. But the

Chamber was unable to say anything concerning the following three months because the judgment had not become a final judgment. The so-called Turkish Republic of Northern Cyprus nevertheless introduced remedies. Let me make one short remark concerning the rent legislation. Very difficult problems of rent legislation were discussed in cases concerning Austria. It is of course clear that practically all States after the Second World War had very strict rent legislations to protect the tenants. And the issue how you deal with that, with property owners' rights, is vague.

K. Oellers-Frahm: In my view, the basic problem that pilot judgments raise concerns the balance between the individual protection and the handling of the caseload. I think we must be very cautious not to interfere with the "individuality" of the protection mechanism, which, in fact, is the core and the reason of success of the Convention system. I think that pilot judgments can only be balanced with the individual protection aspect if they indicate in a rather detailed manner what exactly the State concerned is expected to do. The example of the first sort of "pilot" decision by the Grand Chamber in 1999 in the Italian cases concerning the length of procedure may be referred to in this context. In implementing the decision, the State concerned, Italy, adopted in fact a law opening a domestic remedy to litigants for compensation in cases of exceeding length of court procedures, however, this remedy did not at all conform to the compensation scale adopted in the jurisprudence of the ECtHR. The consequence was that the cases returned to the ECtHR for redress and adequate compensation. It has, of course, to be admitted, that the *Broniowski* decision is a first, although still insufficient step in the right direction. If pilot judgments remain vague in what the State concerned has to do, we will be confronted with a repetition of what happened in the Italian case. I know, of course, that judgments prescribing in a rather detailed manner what the State concerned is expected to do are not unproblematic in legal terms, but if pilot judgments shall have the effect of helping to solve the problem of systemic Convention violations only a clear decision outlining the guiding parameters for redress will be effective.

M. Smrkolj: I would like to comment on the *Lukenda* judgment and in this respect the situation in Slovenia because I think that the Slovenian example might indicate under which circumstances pilot judgments have the potential to achieve their aim. For Slovenia namely, it was very clear among the lawyers and also among the judges of the Constitutional Court that there was no effective domestic remedy for applicants claiming that their rights were affected due to the length of proceedings. But there was no real will to assert that this was the case and to start a process of changing the legislation; also because for instance the Slovenian Constitutional Court was similarly as the European Court overwhelmed by applications. For now, *Lukenda* has been functioning quite well and has triggered the introduction of new legislation providing for a domestic remedy which entered into force this January and has so far been confirmed by the European Court as having the potential to be effective. However, I would also argue that, since the ECtHR enjoys much credibility and authority among Slovenian lawyers and authorities, which might also be due to the fact that there were hardly any cases regarding Slovenia decided so far, apart from the 200 length of proceedings judgments, and because the problem had already been extensively discussed at that time, any judgment might suffice as an incentive to start the domestic process of changing legislation. The Slovenian case thus might implicate that when it comes to countries where on the contrary the Court does not have such authority or there is no political will or sources to remedy the violations, like Turkey, pilot judgments might not be a sufficient incentive for domestic changes but more political pressure would need to be exercised on those countries.

J. Meyer-Ladewig: Just one short point. I can imagine that it is sometimes difficult to choose the case, the good case for a pilot procedure, because it should be a case which has not very much singular, individual features. I heard for instance that the *Broniowski* case was not so good a case because it was singular in a way. And regarding the other applications that are adjourned, these applicants must certainly have the possibility to claim that their case is different, singular, and so that their case has to be decided upon. In pilot judgments – especially when the Court takes its view on necessary general measures into the operative part of the judgment –, the Court does the job that in other cases is done by the Committee of Ministers under Article 46 II. And that was one of the reasons for this procedure because the Committee of Ministers very often didn't know what the result and the consequences of such a judgment would be. And the Court can say that very clearly and in particular when it does so in the operative part.

Concerning the question of *res iudicata*, I am not quite sure whether we can avoid difficulties in all cases. When the State is a party to a procedure, there is no problem. But there are cases with interferences in private relationships between two private parties, tenants, subtenants for instance. And when you allow for a re-opening in such cases you give something to one party, but you take it from the other.

C. Grabenwarter: President *Wildhaber*, you have mentioned a number of problems. I would like to add one further question, the question of identifying systematic problems. You mentioned one example for such a problem, which was relevant in 18 cases. This might not be a lot for a country like Poland, but I would suggest that identifying systematic problems is a process that has several stages. Sometimes the Court gets aware of such a problem only because suddenly a number of cases, which are caused by the systematic problem, are submitted. One should try to find ways to identify the systematic problem before a large number of cases has reached the Court.

The second question is related to the first one. Pilot judgments reduce the workload. I think the situation can and should be compared to the one of national Constitutional Courts. Here in the abstract judicial review a number of procedural mechanisms determine to what extend the cases already pending before the ordinary courts now and those to come are affected by a judgment. Of course it is difficult to make a connection between national procedures and procedures at the level of international law. However, do you – on a political level – think that although it could be difficult, further steps to avoid more applications to be raised during proceedings before the Strasbourg Court should be taken? One suggestion could be that once a decision in a pilot judgment has been reached, no additional application can be submitted to the Strasbourg Court.

S. Oeter: My question is a follow-up to *Christoph Grabenwarter*'s question. I think there is not only the question what is really the systemic deficiency. What puzzles me is: which systemic deficiency is really adequate for that type of a pilot judgment mentioned by President *Wildhaber*? As you yourself, President *Wildhaber*, and also Professor *Frowein* made clear, the issue of systemic deficiency or structural deficiency is a very old problem and the Court in a whole series of judgments has always made explicit that there are aspects of the case which go much beyond the individual case. So the Court has lived with that problem of systemic deficiency already for decades. And I see here a clear reason for the *Broniowski* case where the Court knew that there were 80.000 applications, with a kind of avalanche of applications in behind. If we don't tackle the problem, the members of the Court

Discussion Following the Presentation by Luzius Wildhaber

knew, we will be exploded. Is that really the rationale for going to the pilot judgment type of case, is it only this pragmatic reasoning? Is it the fact that there is a kind of potential avalanche of applications or is there more in behind, perhaps a systematic reflection of the role of the Court? What are the types of cases, the types of systemic deficiencies where you really go to that formal pilot judgment procedure? Because I think it's obvious, also in the recent case practice, that not every systemic deficiency leads to that pilot judgment type of decision.

R. Wolfrum: May I join in this question. Going to different instruments in this issue, the question of systematic violation of human rights is an issue which comes before the human rights treaty bodies: could one borrow from their approach although they don't have pilot judgments, for example from the Committee against Racial Discrimination, which would consider these cases an issue to enact the so-called urgent procedure, which has particular ramifications and in particular requires the States parties to report more frequently and *ad hoc*. Therefore, one may perhaps try to come up with a comparison between the two approaches.

D. Milner: The issue of pilot judgments is one that was considered by the Reflection Group of the Steering Committee of Human Rights, which met for the first time last week. There were few firm conclusions drawn on the procedure, in particular because the representative of the Registry of the Court made clear that it was still evolving and developing; even within the Court, it was unclear exactly what its scope and application were or could become. Perhaps the only conclusion the Reflection Group did clearly draw was that it didn't seem to be necessary for the procedure to be implemented through an amendment to the Convention. The representative of the Registry also mentioned that the Court had in mind the possibility of codifying the procedure in the rules of court, once its definition had become clearer. This highlighted a chicken and egg-sort of problem, because at the moment, not knowing exactly what the procedure would involve, agents were perhaps a little reluctant to accept that the cases being communicated to them should form the beginning of the pilot judgment procedure. On the other hand, without further experience, it would be difficult to determine and define the contours and substance of the procedure.

One distinction that was partially developed during the Reflection Group's meeting was between the sort of situation where the systemic problem defines the scope of the overall problem and the sort of situation where the systemic problem could throw up a potentially limitless number of cases. And perhaps the *Bug River* case and the Italian length of proceeding case are examples of this. For the *Bug River*, there are a certain limited number of people who are affected by the systemic problem. On the other hand, if you are talking about length of proceedings in Italy, well, the number of people affected depends on how many people go to court and find their cases delayed.

P. Mahoney: I will try to help President *Wildhaber* by attempting to give some of the answers to some of the questions. Personally, I do not see why the pilot-judgment procedure should be limited to legislative schemes as has been suggested – that is to say, legislative schemes which apply to large categories of persons and where the allegation is that either the terms of the legislation or the way in which it has been operated give rise to a violation of the Convention. I would not exclude that it could also apply to length of proceedings cases. If a judgment finds, as in *Bottazzi v. Italy* ([GC] ECHR 1999-V), that an administrative practice exists as a result of which the civil justice system is incapable in the country concerned of providing litigants with a trial within a reasonable time, the Court has in effect exhausted its role. It has identified a category of human-rights violations existing within the national legal order. What on earth is the use of the Strasbourg Court continuing to take to judgment, scrutinising the individual facts and assessing the specific relief to be afforded in hundreds, perhaps thousands of cases that do not contribute in any real way to raising the level of human rights protection in Europe? When *Bottazzi* was adjudicated on, there were 14.000 applications from Italy complaining about the excessive length of civil proceedings, which were stocked in a room. These applications had not even been registered because the Registry did not have the staff to deal with them. They were just stored in a room and kept there. When legislation (the Pinto Law) was finally enacted in Italy to introduce a domestic remedy, the Registry hired, over the six weeks of the summer break, a team of temporary secretaries, who had to type out 14.000 letters informing these applicants that they were now obliged to exhaust this new remedy (to complain about the length of civil proceedings) in Italy. This is contrary to the usual rule on exhaustion of domestic remedies. The usual rule is that applicants are only obliged to exhaust such remedies as exist at the time they lodge their application. However, in order to resolve a practical problem, the Court exceptionally held that applicants were obliged to exhaust a remedy which was created after the lodging of the application.

Article 46 of the Convention quite clearly may give rise to an obligation on the respondent State to take general measures to amend legislation or change an administrative practice and not simply to take individual measures granting relief to the particular applicant in the particular case. I cannot identify any legal bar on the Court's specifying, in so far as this is appropriate and possible on the facts, the concrete consequences of that obligation under Article 46 in a judgment finding a violation and even inserting that conclusion in the operative provisions. I do not understand why the Court's proceeding in such a manner in appropriate circumstances is in any way contrary to the Convention or to the rule of the binding effect of judgments. As is quite apparent if one reads the judgment in *Broniowski*, the government were simply called on to ensure that all *Bug River* ex-property owners, not just the applicant but all persons who were in the same position as Mr. *Broniowski* under the contested legislation, should be able to enjoy their right of property as provided for under the Convention *or else be given equivalent relief in lieu*. So the government were afforded a large degree of flexibility as to how they should implement the judgment and fulfil their obligation under Article 46. Whatever the Polish Agent may say, the Polish government were given considerable freedom as to how they executed the judgment in *Broniowski*.

The *Broniowski* judgment essentially contained two elements on the issue of execution. The government were told: firstly, you have to eliminate the source of the violation, that is for the future; and, secondly, you must provide a remedy for past prejudice that has been suffered by not only the individual applicant but also all the other 80.000 *Bug River* claimants adversely affected by the systemic violation found. Both of these things the Polish government did indeed do in *Broniowski*. The Polish government enacted new legislation which offered cash compensation for the property that had been lost, in addition to the previously sole possibility of bidding in public auctions for sale of government property. Secondly, they gave a written undertaking acknowledging that although there was no national case law existing, certain remedies within the Polish legal system could be used for claiming financial compensation for non-material loss suffered because of the defective functioning of the contested legislative *Bug River* scheme; they agreed not to contest before the Polish courts the fact that these remedies could be used for that purpose within the Polish legal system.

All the other *Bug River* cases pending before the Strasbourg Court had previously been suspended awaiting the outcome of the *Broniowski* case. Following the measures of execution of the *Broniowski* judgment, the applicants in all these suspended cases were told to go back to the national legal system and use this new legislation for obtaining compensation for the lost property and these existing remedies for past prejudice. A few applicants did that but then came straight back to Strasbourg a second time in order to complain about the low level of the financial compensation that they had received under the new legislation. They received only 20 per cent, not 100 per cent compensation for the value of the property they had lost. They argued that this was not enough. They therefore wanted the Strasbourg Court to find a violation of the right of property by reason of the new legislation. I have here a decision of the Court, dating from 4 December of this year, where these cases were struck out, precisely on the basis that the matter had been resolved. Consequently, two years after the friendly settlement judgment in *Broniowski*, "the matter" of the malfunctioning of the *Bug River* legislative scheme has been "resolved" – not just for Mr. *Broniowski*, but for all the 80.000 Bug River claimants concerned.

It is true that this approach of striking out on the basis of the full resolution of the matter cannot necessarily be adopted in relation to the length–of-proceedings cases, because, if *Bottazzi* is taken as an example, it is clear that while the Italians have introduced a remedy to obtain compensation for past prejudice, it is far from sure that they have removed the source of the violation. Thus, in the Italian length-of-civil-proceedings cases subsequent to the Pinto Law, the applications were struck out, not on the basis that the matter had been resolved, but for non-exhaustion of domestic remedies.

My conclusion is therefore that the pilot-judgment procedure could be used in length of proceedings cases where there is perceived to be a generalized problem, but the follow-up cases suspended awaiting the outcome of the pilot judgment could not necessarily be struck out on the basis that the matter had been resolved.

When is there room for pilot judgments? The point has rightly been made that the pilot-judgment procedure is not a miracle solution. It has to be used in a flexible way. The *Broniowski* judgment makes it clear that this kind of approach is suitable when there is a risk of an avalanche of similar cases being lodged with the Strasbourg Court. If the position is simply that there is a general problem in the country concerned, then what is needed is what is sometimes called a "judgment of principle", which may have consequences elsewhere. But, although the judgment may well settle the issue for many other persons in a similar situation in the country concerned (hence a "judgment of principle"), it will not necessarily have the characteristics of a "pilot judgment" in the *Broniowski* sense. A pilot judgment in this sense is called for when there are already a number of applications pending or there is a risk of a flood of similar applications being lodged. The object, as *Luzius Wildhaber* said, is to prevent that flood. The pilot-judgment procedure does not necessarily reduce the work for the Court as regards the applications that are already pending. But it will certainly prevent a situation such as the one regarding the enjoyment of property rights by Greek Cypriots in Northern Cyprus. There are 1.400 such cases pending. Are all these cases to be taken to judgment? An actuarial study is required in each case to calculate the value of the house or the business in issue. For example, if it was a hotel, the question will arise: was it near the sea, did it have a good view, did it have a restaurant, how much money was the business likely to earn? If such a calculation is going to have to be carried out in all those 1.400 cases, the Strasbourg Court will become a property-claims commission for Northern Cyprus. Is it that what the ECtHR and its 47 international judges are there for? At least the prospect of 80.000 *Bug River* cases in Strasbourg has been avoided. That is the value of the pilot-judgment procedure.

In conclusion, I agree that the pilot-judgment procedure does not address a new problem. Rent-control cases have existed before, for example Judgments of principle have been delivered before. What was new in *Broniowski* was that the Court sought to develop a practical mechanism for reducing the flow of repetitive applications and the work involved in processing them. It may not work. Not all governments will necessarily be as cooperative as the Polish government. Also it may be that a solution of the problem is not immediately feasible or available. The Northern Cyprus problem, for example, is one that has bedevilled the world and the UN for the last 35 years or so. The idea that a Chamber of the Court in Strasbourg would end this intractable political problem with a legal direction to the Turkish government to settle everything within three months was doubtless rather unrealistic. Evidently, in each case the Court itself has to make a realistic assessment of whether, on the particular facts, the pilot-judgment procedure is susceptible of producing workable results. This will not always be so and it is by no means a miracle solution. Thank you.

R. Bernhardt: I am a little more sceptical in respect of pilot judgments than my friend *Paul Mahoney*, mainly for legal reasons. I agree that the

Broniowski case was an adequate case for this procedure. I still have doubts whether it is satisfactory to have the statements concerning systemic deficiencies in the operative part of the judgment. These statements could be left to the reasoning of the judgment; this could avoid some difficulties in the future. But there are other problems connected with pilot judgments. It can hardly be doubted that third States confronted with similar systemic problems are not bound by a judgment against another state. The third state must remain free not to follow a pilot judgment. The *Bug River* situation was in my opinion unique, and the pilot judgment solution was in that case adequate. It may also be useful in other areas, but it should be applied in a careful manner.

K. Doehring: In the land reform case before the Court, dealing with the expropriation of property by the GDR government only the *Maltzan* case came before the Court. Many arguments of the other applicants have never been heard. And I think they didn't have the opportunity to bring new arguments before the Court in a hard case, particularly arguments which are not in conformity perhaps with the first applicant in the *Maltzan* case. And how to convince the Court with arguments, a Court which is not prepared to hear the case. And so I think pilot judgments may have some justification, but often even in the oral procedure, there may be brought arguments, which have not been brought forward in the written argument because nobody knows whether the judges have read the paper or not, but only with oral procedures you can stress some arguments again and again. If one does not have the opportunity to do that, then I think a fair trial is in danger.

L. Wildhaber: Thank you very much. This was a most interesting discussion showing all the ambiguities of the pilot judgment and all the implicit assumptions on what the Court should do without necessarily always spelling them out. And it was in a sense a very illustrative and very good discussion to demonstrate where the problems are. So, thank you very much. It was also a typical Western European discussion. In other words, we looked at the problem as all of us taught the problem of human rights in courses. We stop when the Supreme or Constitutional Court has spoken, or maybe when the European Court has spoken. Then it is over, and the problem is solved. However with the new Member States that is not a realistic approach. We would have to look far more to execution, to what really happens to the chances of judgments being executed, and to the good faith in the execution. When all this is said, we have to go back to the length of proceedings cases and confess that it all began with Western European States that resisted an effective execution for something like 20 years. Do you know the film Divorzio all'italiana? Where the wife takes a lover who is supposed to kill the husband and then she takes off with the lover. The last scene shows her on a yacht; there is a young man helping on the yacht and you see how she gets into physical contact with the new man and you know that the lover who replaced the husband will suffer the same fate as the husband. It is very understandable that you encounter this phenomenon of the Divorzio all'italiana given the length of Italian proceedings; that is an obvious way of getting a divorce.

I shall try to go through the remarks, but cannot answer to everything.

Your initial question, *Erika de Wet*, about the applicability of the pilot judgment procedure to the reasonable time requirement has been aptly answered by *Paul Mahoney*. Again it is all a question of execution. It is not only a question of whether the pilot judgment procedure lends itself to addressing these issues, it is also an issue of the willingness of governments and states to respond in a meaningful way. And that is probably the most fundamental problem of the pilot judgment procedure. *Paul Mahoney* has described how the binding force of pilot judgments and the direct effect on other cases have played out in the *Broniowski* case. Whether we should apply the notion of *res iudicata* for ECtHR cases by analogy to other cases is doubtful to me. I do not think we should. We after all issue only declaratory judgments, which must be executed on the domestic level. But of course, our judgments are judgments that should normally be applied in analogous cases in third States. Mr. *Bernhardt* is right in pointing out that under the Convention a judgment is binding only on the States parties to a specific procedure. However, some cases are obviously meant to be extended to all the Member States, such as the homosexuality cases, the *Marckx* case about the status of illegitimate children, the *Christine Goodwin* case on transsexualism. Some may call such cases judgments of principle. I have never quite understood what a judgment of principle is. It is perhaps not a hazard that our Court has never identified cases as being judgments of principle. The good administration of justice requires that similar facts be handled in the same way and under the same rules. In that sense, judgments have the force of precedent. This follows from the equality before the law and the coherence and the consistency of the case law of a court. A European Court might be accused of double standards if it tried to apply a homosexuality judgment to one State only and not to others. So there must be a force of precedent, although the Court can overrule itself, as it has done in the name of an evolutive jurisprudence (some would even want to speak of a dynamic jurisprudence). The rule must nevertheless be that judgments are to be applied to other similar factual situations.

Anne Peters spoke of atypical pilot judgments. She asked whether they apply only against new Member States. The Court would never wish to be caught at saying something like this. The time had simply come to begin experimenting with pilot judgments. The Court is still in an experimental stage, if we may put it somewhat bluntly. One does not always know all the answers in advance, certainly not in an international court, where the factual problems that come up are so different. Surely, the pilot judgment procedure must be applied against all States. It so happened that the first two typical pilot judgments went against Poland, which may have been too much of a good thing. But it was illustrative enough; the Polish government was very willing to cooperate in the *Broniowski* case. They were less willing in the *Hutten-Czapska* case, arguing that the case did not lend itself to the pilot judgment procedure. Among other things, their view was that the *Hutten-Czapska* case dealt with the relationship between landlords and tenants and this was a central issue of what is commonly called social policy. Should that really be decided by a court? Should that not be decided by the democratically elected instances of a State, the government and the parliament, always provided that we can qualify that State as a real democracy? For that reason alone pilot judgments have got to go against all the States. The *Scordino* case defined more or less where the Court would accept execution on the domestic level and would not interfere. It handled the case the traditional way, did not adjourn cases and did not give more specific instructions. *Anne Peters* called the case a judgment of principle. Of course, if the Court knew what was meant with the notion of a judgment of principle, it would owe it to everybody to identify those judgments.

What happens to parallel applicants and applications? Unless the Court adjourns them, the procedure is hardly a pilot judgment procedure. There is always a close connection with the enormity of the Court's workload. At the time of the *Broniowski* case, not everybody had the same opinions as to what a pilot judgment would mean in subsequent cases. I think there was agreement that subsequent cases could come up again before the Court, after Poland would have accepted the compensation scheme. Afterwards, it works pretty much the way *Paul Mahoney* has described it. The Court will look at some of the leading Polish cases and will define what it considers as a sufficient percentage of the compensation that can be requested and then this will be applicable to the other cases and it will for practical purposes determine the merits of these cases in the Strasbourg system.

The Court has issued by now not hundreds but thousands of cases on length of proceedings. There are burning issues that are waiting such as the Kurdish and the Chechen cases that admittedly concern very grave violations of human rights. Is it correct to invest the Court's energies in the length of proceedings cases and ask whether five years before two instances is too long or is not long enough, whereas priority should be given to cases such as the Chechen and Kurdish? My clear answer is that this is not the right way of doing things. Nor should the Court have to decide cases over and over again that have been conclusively decided. There should be a better recognition and acceptance of priorities. Could the Court on its own decide what the priorities should be and would not a legal basis be needed? It would certainly be most desirable if a better legal basis existed. It is just foreseeable that the Court will hardly get such a basis in the next years, and it will be the Court's challenge to decide whether or not to react on its own.

Some of you have spoken about the Cypriot cases. There has been a considerable amount of intrusiveness and disrespect of the independence of the Court in connection with these cases. Before the referendum on the Kofi Annan peace plan, there was an orchestrated movement of bringing cases to the Court, obviously in the hope of getting higher indemnities than a claims commission from Northern Cyprus might award. I heard with great interest that the Cypriot problem might be submitted to the Court of Justice. This Court is known as a court of economics. I trust the Court of Justice and am sure it will decide wisely.

I think I want to conclude with a remark about it being doubtful that all the pilot judgments will indeed be executed by the States concerned. The Court should not look into that, I suppose. It is the Committee of Ministers which looks into that. The Court has often had an easier life because it did not have to. But there is indeed a problem with pilot judgments, the basis of which cannot be found directly in the Convention about whether States will always be willing to cooperate fully. Look at my own country, Switzerland. So the Court recently issued a judgment *Ünal Tekeli v. Turkey* and stated that the wife had the right to continue keeping her maiden name in the name of the Convention. Both Turkey and Switzerland are deliberating about changing their civil law. Would Switzerland accept a pilot judgment? Well, of course we would say that we are very unique and have a referendum against every statute. Statutes voted by parliament are actually only draft bills, no more than that. If there is a referendum vote and if the people do not want the draft bill, it becomes politically very difficult to turn down the vote of the people because of a pilot (or other) judgment. Such a reaction might occur in different ways in different countries. It is a touchy issue, and so we are still in an experimental stage. I shall stop here and thank you very much.

Fair Trial and Excessive Length of Proceedings as Focal Points of the ECtHR's Increasing Caseload

Mark Villiger[1]

A. Introduction

My topic completes the series of presentations on how to deal with the great number of applications facing the Court. It identifies one group of cases "responsible" for the huge back-log, i.e., cases concerning the fairness of proceedings under Article 6 in general, and the length of proceedings in particular. I shall attempt to circumscribe the difficulties with the help of some statistics, and then put forward some proposals how to deal with these problems.

B. Where Lies the Problem? Some Statistics

Where lies the problem? It is considered that issues under Article 6 of the Convention (concerning access to Court, fair trial, speedy length of proceedings) contribute substantially to the Court's workload, and that cases concerning length of proceedings, since often they cannot be declared inadmissible *de plano*, prove to be particularly time-consuming.

What do the statistics tell us on these cases? Starting point is the current number of pending cases, i.e. 103.964 applications, on 3 December 2007. This is the workload awaiting the Court. A daunting figure which

---

[1] These opinions are personal and in no way reflect the views of the European Court of Human Rights in Strasbourg.

is indeed the reason why we are here today trying to find a way out. At its current cruising speed (the Court deals with about 30.000 cases a year), it would take the Court three years to deal with this backlog. However, as you can imagine, there are constantly new cases flowing in. Just to give you a further anecdotal statistic which is nevertheless telling: the Court receives about 1.000 letters a day. In other words: approximately every two minutes somebody in Europe is writing to the Court.

As regards the statistics concerning our topic, you can see on my outline that on 3 December 2007, of this total backlog of approximately 100.000 cases, some 33.920 raise an issue, *inter alia*, under Article 6 of the Convention. Of these Article 6 applications, about 47 per cent of the cases (15.989) have been earmarked as Committee cases, i.e. they appear provisionally to be inadmissible cases which can be dealt with by a Committee of three judges. Conversely, a slight majority of 53 per cent of the cases (17.931) are to be dealt with in a Section, i.e., it is assumed that potentially there might be a problem in these cases. This ratio of Committee and Section cases is particularly striking, since lawyers are instructed *a priori* not to bring a case before a Section if it is inadmissible.

Let us scrutinise those cases which concern the *length of civil or criminal proceedings*. Here you will see on the outline that a total of 8.566 such cases are pending. This is roughly one third of the total number of cases concerning Article 6. However, among these cases, 1.515, i.e., about 22 per cent only, are to be dealt with in Committee. The majority of these cases, 7.051 raise serious issues to be examined more closely in a Section and most likely raise an issue under the Convention.

Let me draw three conclusions from these statistics:

1. Complaints under Article 6 provide for the lion's share of the Court's work-load, about one third of the total number of pending applications;

2. It is not possible to say that a large part of these applications are inadmissible. To the contrary, slightly more than half of Article 6 cases are earmarked for a Section, i.e. potentially they contain a violation of the Convention;

3. Most length of proceedings cases are not *a priori* inadmissible;

On the whole, I find these figures quite alarming!

Incidentally, one may wonder why it is that applicants prefer to complain under Article 6 of the Convention. I can only offer you my personal opinion in this respect. I suspect it has to do with the inherent structure of judicial proceedings. You see, *ex hypothesi* there will always be a winner and a loser. In civil proceedings, the loser among the two private parties will certainly wish to become a winner – if necessary in last resort in Strasbourg. And in criminal cases, one party – the accused – will often also wish to test the fairness of the proceedings (and quite often their length) at the ECtHR.

C. How to Deal with the Problem?

Having identified the problem – or to be more precise: having *confirmed* the problem which the *hosts* of this Workshop have *identified* – let me address some seven proposals which aim specifically at helping the Court reduce its backlog in respect of these cases.

1. Drafting Techniques

First, quite an efficient way of getting rid of this backlog is by adapting briefer, more precise drafting techniques. Reduce the number of pages per case by 50 per cent, and the Court's Registry can produce twice as many cases! Well, not quite. The shorter a text is to be, the longer a lawyer drafting the decision or judgment will need to decide what is relevant, and what can be left out. Remember Bismarck's words to his generals, I quote: "today I do not have time to be brief" (*Meine Herren Generäle, ich habe heute keine Zeit mich kurz zu fassen*). Moreover, *ex hypothesi* length of proceedings cases, encompassing many years, for instance, of social proceedings cases, accumulate masses of events, which may to some extent be relevant for a judgment on the due or undue length of the proceedings. Bear in mind, too, that lawyers are under considerable pressure to produce a sufficient number of draft judgments and decisions. There comes a moment in a lawyer's calculation where he or she will prefer not to lose even more time shortening a case, and instead commence with the next one.

But the underlying thought must be correct and should be vigorously pursued. In practical terms, lawyers in the Court's registry are requested to be precise and state only the absolutely necessary of the facts, and are taught in workshops how to do so.

2. Grouping Committee Cases

Second, another simple technique in the Registry may have a considerable effect, i.e., grouping Committee cases. Such cases concern inadmissible applications in respect of all Convention guarantees. Committee cases are prepared by a lawyer, quality checked by a further lawyer, and immediately given to a Committee of three judges which must unanimously accept the proposal of inadmissibility. Otherwise they go to a Section.

For each Committee case the lawyer prepares a proposal of maximum one page (regrettably, there are a lot of exceptions), in which the salient points are summarised. Everything must turn around the ground of inadmissibility, explanations on the merits of the case are unnecessary.

The technique is then to group a number of these applications, say: all concerning non-exhaustion, prepare a list of them, and next to each application state in maximum half a sentence what remedy was *not* employed. Facts are no longer mentioned. One can prepare lists of cases concerning fourth-instance issues, i.e. complaints about the incorrect outcome of proceedings, and state next to each application only the topic of the proceedings (i.e., dispute among neighbours, conviction for speeding, etc.).

Let me mention two caveats. One, such lists are very much a matter of trust which judges have in the lawyers, for instance, that the case, deemed to be fourth instance, does not in fact concern more. It is understandable if some judges have hesitations in this respect. The other caveat: it is not always easy for lawyers to *find* great numbers of applications all raising the one single issue – and no other ones!

3. Encouraging Friendly Settlements

Third, over the years, the different proposals made on how to reduce the Court's backlog have suggested more frequent use of friendly settlements. In a friendly settlement, the government as a rule offers a sum of money and the applicant withdraws the application. Traditionally, there is no determination of a violation of the Convention. Occasionally, the government goes further and offers to propose new legislation, or even admits a violation. As a result of a friendly settlement, the case is struck off the Court's list of cases.

Clearly, negotiating a friendly settlement may be time-consuming, involving at times lengthy discussions between the parties: it may even be more "productive" immediately to draft a judgment. However, friendly settlements can play a useful role in cases of standard violations, e.g. length of proceedings. In every such case governments should automatically consider the possibility of a friendly settlement under regular terms in all such cases. This would really assist the Court tremendously in dealing with these often time-consuming cases.

May I add that there must always be the possibility of negotiating friendly settlements between the parties even if this looks like a waste of time. There is currently a Working Party in the Court examining how to be more pro-active in this respect. In my view, the highest Court of Europe must have some policy in bringing about "Win-Win" situations in contentious proceedings.

4. Unilateral Statements

Fourth, if a friendly settlement cannot be reached because the applicant refuses the government's offer, the Court may in standard cases, e.g. length of proceedings, be willing to accept a unilateral statement by the government. The latter will offer a sum of money and will acknowledge a violation, for instance, of Article 6 of the Convention. If the applicant refuses this offer, the Court will accept it in the applicant's name. Having accepted the offer for the applicant, the Court will then strike the case out of its list.

Unilateral declarations stem from the consideration that applicants often erroneously refuse the government's offer, namely because they fail to see that there are no *other* issues in the case; or because they claim some astronomical sum of money.

5. Prioritising Cases (fast-tracking)

Fifth, let us look at a novel proposal, that of prioritising cases. Currently, the Court gives priority to cases if they concern danger to life and limb, mainly in expulsion cases, and in other exceptional cases such as very aged, or very ill, or very young applicants.

A Working Party in the Court has recently made proposals whereby priority should be granted more frequently in cases which reflect a general problem (mainly pilot cases) and cases of major general interest, i.e. cases which have major repercussions on the domestic legal orders; inter-State cases.

These proposals are sound, though they are not really dramatic. But the Court's Working Party is considering further, more drastic ways of prioritising applications. This is an interesting development which I would briefly wish to share with you.

In particular, the question may be asked: why should a valid application, raising a serious issue under the Convention, wait until all other inadmissible cases before it or even standard violation cases (e.g., length of proceedings) have been decided? Why should such cases not be put on the fast track and overtake all other "unimportant" (in inverted commas) ones.

Of course, fast-tracking applications may not get rid of more cases, but it ensures that the important ones are dealt with fast. Clearly, a list of criteria needs to be prepared which carefully define and establish the grounds of fast-tracking. Naturally, the Court must enjoy a certain leeway in prioritising certain cases.

Let me mention some difficulties. With the growth of the number of "important" cases, the waiting period for the "other" applications could soon become agonisingly long. If more cases are fast-tracked than are actually dealt with by the Court in one year, the remaining cases would never have a chance to be examined. Moreover, distinguishing one group from the other would require careful study of all incoming case-files which may lay an additional burden on the Court and its Registry immediately after an application had been filed. Furthermore, imagine if after countless years of waiting, the case-file of a so-called clearly inadmissible case is opened and found to contain a major violation of the Convention. Finally, the proposal calls into question the principle that individuals filing applications are treated equally before the Convention – for which reason the applications should be dealt with in order of their arrival.

The Reflection Group of the Steering Committee in Human Rights of the Council of Europe last week dealt with this particular matter and considered it worth pursuing.

6. Protocol 14–Threshold

A sixth proposal can be found in the Protocol No. 14 and concerns the amendment of Article 35 para. 3 by introducing a new ground of inadmissibility, namely that:

"the applicant has not suffered a significant disadvantage, unless respect for human rights as defined in the Convention and the Protocols thereto requires an examination of the application on the merits and provided that no case may be rejected on this ground which has not been duly considered by a domestic tribunal."

If I am not mistaken, the case *Koumoutsea and others v. Greece* lay behind his proposal, if not, it is a good example for the type of complaints that the proposal wishes to "catch" and declare inadmissible.

Koumoutsea was an administrative Judge in Greece. As such he was entitled to a car to drive to work. If the service cars were not used (e.g. because of public transport), judges could ask for a sum of money as compensation. In the *Koumoutsea* case, that Judge requested back payment of 52,82 Euros for not having used his service car. Before the Greek courts these proceedings lasted nine years, during the proceedings the Judge died and the widow and his children took over in the proceedings. Subsequently the Strasbourg Court found a violation of Article 6 para. 1 of the Convention – how could it not? – of the requirement of speedy proceedings.

The reasoning behind the new ground of inadmissibility in Protocol No. 14 is to prevent precisely such cases as *Koumoutsea v. Greece* in future.

This new ground of admissibility, which will exclude applications otherwise leading to a Convention violation, is particularly suitable for Article 6 cases, in particular the length of civil proceedings. (It is hardly conceivable that this ground of inadmissibility is applied in criminal cases.) It has a classic filtering function. It allows the Court to devote more time to "important" cases, both as regards the applicant and the European public order. The two safeguards – respect for human rights and the previous examination by a domestic tribunal – ensure that cases which warrant an examination of the merits are not rejected.

It is as yet unclear what gains in productivity this new admissibility criterion would enable – possibly another 5-10 per cent. However, in my view, the low gain in productivity is not the only issue to be considered here. In qualitative terms, it may be assumed that the criterion will have a powerful symbolic function by further strengthening the conviction among States that the Court should only deal with "important" cases.

If Protocol No. 14 does not come about, in my view a future Protocol should pick up this proposal, develop it even further and employ inadmissibility grounds along the lines of the Federal Constitutional Court. According to subparas. 2 (a) and (b) of Section 93 (a) of the German Federal Constitutional Court Act, a constitutional complaint is only accepted if it has fundamental constitutional significance and – I am putting it simply here – if the complainant would suffer an especially grave disadvantage if no decision is given. So the test before the Federal Constitutional Court is actually inverse to the one proposed by Protocol No. 14.

7. New Convention on Remedies

Finally, seventh, I wish to draw attention to a proposal made by the Deputy Secretary General at the San Marino Conference in March 2007 to follow up the Report of the Wise Persons. It was suggested in particular to adopt a new Council of Europe Convention containing obligations for Member States as regards the availability, functioning and effectiveness of domestic remedies, in particular concerning excessive length of proceeding cases.

This proposal goes back to the Committee of Ministers' Recommendation of 2004, Recommendation (2004) 6 on the improvement of domestic remedies. Therein it was recommended that Member States, "ascertain ... that domestic remedies exist for anyone with an arguable complaint of a violation of the Convention, and that these remedies are effective", that the Member States "where necessary set up effective remedies, in order to avoid repetitive cases being brought before the Court" and that "they pay particular attention ... to the existence of effective remedies in cases of an arguable complaint concerning the excessive length of judicial proceedings".

This recommendation and the proposal of the Wise Persons of 2006 to improve domestic remedies for redressing violations of the Convention led as the next step to the above-mentioned suggestion. Indeed, the above-mentioned reflection group of the Council of Europe's Steering Committee for Human Rights examined, *inter alia*, this proposal last week.

What is to be said of a Convention expressing itself on domestic remedies in length of proceedings cases? Clearly, it is *a priori* a most laudable project. Any extension of the protection of human rights on the domestic level must be applauded, not least in the light of the governing principle of subsidiarity. Put differently, if all the States had efficient domestic remedies, the Court would not have a backlog. If such a Convention leads to less applications, this would justify its existence. Of course, even in the most optimistic of assumptions, any assistance provided by such a Convention would only be in the far future, i.e. long term. But even that should not deter the Steering Committee from pursuing this project. However, there are a number of caveats which come to mind.

It is interesting to note that the proposal does not aim at a new Protocol additional to the European Human Rights Convention – which is the usual instrument to expand the Convention guarantees or reform its procedures. Rather, a new Convention on domestic remedies is envisaged. Perhaps it is hoped that because a Convention is binding (as opposed to a Resolution of the Committee of Ministers), it will put pressure on Member States to introduce such remedies? Obviously, the new Convention would come to stand parallel to the European Human Rights Convention, but would not, I imagine, intend to change it. But there is still the problem of *lex posterior derogat legi priori*, and equally of *lex specialis derogat legi generali*, and in particular the impact of the later Convention on the Court's case law on precisely such remedies.

Indeed, the biggest question-mark of all is: what will be the position of such landmark cases of the Court as *Kudla v. Poland*, requiring precisely such remedies in length of proceedings cases? Will such a new Convention not undermine the obligation of States to comply with Article 13 in combination with Article 6 in their interpretation by the Strasbourg case law?

Conclusion

I set out the problems before you and offered some first indications how in my own view their resolution should occur. While none of these means provide a *panacea* to cure all problems, I do believe that taken together there is much potential among them.

On the whole I warmly congratulate the hosts for organising this Workshop. The Court is currently enduring what in German finds an appropriate expression: a *Reformstau*, i.e. reform proposals are getting blocked. Yet it is so important for us here today to question these and other proposals, to test them, to put them in order, and to develop a sort of road map which will guide the Court in the next decades.

Discussion Following the Presentation by Mark Villiger

J.A. Frowein: Thank you again, Judge *Villiger*, for the most impressive remarks to the Article 6 cases and the length of procedure cases among them. Let me take up one little issue which really stunned me. You said that the Court system must respect the equality of all applicants and therefore the order in time to deal with the cases must in principle be the order in which the applications were introduced. Let me say in a very blunt way that I fully disagree. Why do I disagree? Of course, the right to individual application is a right of every citizen and every person subject to the jurisdiction of one of the Convention States. In that respect, you have of course equality of all these human beings. But does that mean that what they bring to Strasbourg is equal in the sense that it must be dealt with in the same order of time? Again, let me say: I completely disagree. As regards the application of rules of equality in all our systems, wherever equality exists as a rule of law in constitutions or in Article 14 of the ECHR, we always distinguish between the cases according to the different facts of the cases. And I see no reason whatsoever not to do that with the caseload coming to the Strasbourg Court. In fact, I mean that in that respect there is no distinction between what happened in the European Commission of Human Rights, which I mentioned yesterday, when the wave of Italian length cases came. We all agree that statistically, there will be a violation in probably 90 per cent of all the cases. Nevertheless, the importance of these cases compared with many other cases for the European Human Rights System for the individual applicants, for the system as such was comparatively minor. Therefore, we have dealt with these cases in a special manner. We tried of course to also dispose of them within a reasonable time, not always easy. But I think that the idea of equality among the applicants should not be a reason to prevent the Court from dealing with cases in a similar way as the Commission.

A. Wittling-Vogel: Thank you very much and thank you, Judge *Villiger*, for your presentation. I would like to add some remarks from my own experience with German cases. I think we can say that, considering all the judgments against Germany for violation of the Convention, approximately one-third of them are length of proceeding cases. And I would like to support what you said: from the point of view of the applicant, many of these cases concern primarily not the length of the proceedings, but rather other violations of the Convention. These are applicants who are disappointed that they lost their case on the national level. Then they go to Strasbourg and in the first place, they mention the alleged violation of, for example, Article 5, Article 8, etc. And then they add the complaint about the length of proceedings. The Court very often decides that the primary complaint about the other Articles is inadmissible. And so we deal only with the length of proceeding violation. That is the source of many length of proceeding cases. And in the cases which in the end have to do only with the length of proceedings, for the past year or two we have had a new approach in coordination with the Court. We take a brief look at the case and if we can't add valid arguments to justify the length of proceedings, we ask the Court for a proposal for a friendly settlement. The Court always makes a proposal and the government always accepts the proposal. If the applicant does not accept, which happens quite often because applicants very often have a different notion of how much money they should get, we proceed to unilateral declarations. Our government declares and informs the Court that we accept that there has been a violation of human rights, of Article 6 in these cases. Then we declare that we are ready to pay a sum of money to the applicant. In Germany, we take the proposal of the Court for the friendly settlement and deduct 10 per cent. We deduct 10 per cent because the applicant gets not only the money, but also the declaration that his or her human rights have been violated. We already have two judgments where the Court has accepted that procedure. And of course, what we are doing and what we must do as a parallel measure is to work on new legislation concerning length of proceeding cases, to create a remedy against excessive length of proceedings. I would like to add something concerning a new Convention on domestic remedies because we discussed it last week in Strasbourg in the new reflection group. For me, I think the last point you mentioned is the most important. What could be the effect of such a new Convention? I am a bit reluctant about it because I imagine that we would have a new Convention text, and then we have all the governments which have problems with length of proceeding cases. Will they ratify this new Convention? And if they don't, if we have only, let's say, two-thirds of all Member States ratify this new Convention, what impact would that have on the case law of the Court and on Article 13 of the Convention? Now we have Article 13 of the Convention and we have the case law of the Court, the *Kudla* case and all the other cases, for Germany the *Sürmeli* case. This is quite a solid base – knowing what is right and what is wrong as far as Article 13 is concerned. But if we start to work on a new Convention, every State has the possibility to say: I won't ratify. And this could weaken the position of the Court, the case law of the Court, and Article 13; indeed, it could undermine the system we have today. This is why I am reluctant about this new Convention and as far as I understand, the reflection group as a whole was not very enthusiastic about this point last week. Thank you very much.

J. Meyer-Ladewig: A few words concerning the prioritizing of cases, a most interesting topic. I think it is a normal procedure for each and every court, national court and international court to decide first on priority cases, that is self-evident and that works. But the higher the workload, the backlog, the more important becomes this question of priority. When we see the growing backlog, the decision of the Court which cases shall be dealt with as priority cases comes near to the discussion we had yesterday because the result may be that there are some no-priority cases that will be never dealt with or so late that the decision is not of interest any more. Nevertheless, I feel it's absolutely necessary to find a way to decide priority cases. This is done and this should be done more and more. I am grateful, Judge *Villiger*, that you mentioned the new admissibility criterion in the 14th Protocol. You estimated it covers 5 to 10 per cent of the cases. I agree with that. I don't think that there will be many cases. But nevertheless, this new criterion is a chance for the Court to develop it and to find a good solution with it. The provision is a bit difficult to read and it has become more and more difficult during the discussions of the 14th Protocol. But nevertheless, there is a chance to perhaps find a new way. Thank you.

D. Milner: Yes, many of Judge *Villiger*'s proposals were discussed to some extent by the Reflection Group last week. I am neither going to cover all of what Judge *Villiger* said nor all 67 proposals that were considered by the reflection group, but instead mention only a few specific points. On friendly settlements, one problem that emerged was a great diversity in attitude and practice between government agents as regards how they should be dealing with applicants. Some agents, for example, were very reluctant to take any direct contact with applicants. This seemed to be a reflection of the legal and administrative culture from which they came. Others considered it to be entirely natural, something they did as a matter of course whenever they thought it could be useful, and never encountered any difficulties. One solution that the Group considered might help was for the Court to give guidance on the circumstances and manner in which the agents could and should be approaching applicants with a view to negotiating a friendly settlement. Relatedly, I think that Ms. *Wittling-Vogel* mentioned this, it was observed that friendly settlements are often rejected because the applicant's expectations of an eventual award are wildly unrealistic. One of the experts on the group said that this was sometimes of the order of hundreds of times what the Court tended to conclude in similar cases. The initial discussions were directed towards the possibility of some form of guidelines, whether from the Court or elsewhere –, the Court could be the most appropriate body in terms of having the knowledge, but the Registry were reluctant to engage in this sort of exercise, because of complications such as the differences in purchasing power between different States and the fact that any guidelines would become outdated over time as a result of inflation. What the Court Registry is now considering, in the course of its ongoing development of the HUDOC system, is to introduce a mechanism for searching the database to ascertain patterns in the awards of just satisfaction in particular types of cases. This would be a tool that could be used by applicants and their lawyers to have an idea of what they might get, should their application come to a positive conclusion, and whether in the light of this information, they should be accepting any friendly settlement offered by the respondent States' agents or authorities. In this context, it was considered that the longer the applicants have to wait before being approached with a view to a friendly settlement, the more likely they are to have become excited about the prospects of a positive judgment. So there was some consideration of how and whether the respondent States should be informed of certain cases at an earlier stage so that they might have an opportunity to approach applicants at that stage.

The other point I was going to address was a possible new Convention on domestic remedies. A lot has been said about this. I won't address this question in detail, the conclusion of the Reflection Group having been to set the idea aside for the time being. Many principled objections were expressed, as have also been mentioned today. For me one of the most persuasive was the problem of identifying a sufficiently precise definition, even in the Court's case law, of what an effective remedy is. There are principles concerning what it should achieve, but no clear definition for identifying an effective remedy in advance. This leads into the problem of how the Court, or perhaps some other control mechanism, would interpret any domestic remedies introduced under a new

Convention and whether the jurisprudence under a new Convention would be any different from the Court's jurisprudence under Article 13.

A. Peters: I would also like to comment on the question of effective domestic remedies. Would it not be possible for the Court to exploit Article 46 ECHR more? Could it not modify its practice of stating that the choice of the means for redress is left to the Member States as long as these means are effective? In the length of proceeding cases, the Court – as far as I see – accepts either monetary compensation or a type of restitution in natural kind. But I think that for length of proceeding cases, these standard two remedies do not fully fit because natural restitution is not really possible. You can not bring back the lost time, except in cases of a criminal judgment sentencing somebody to jail: here you can reduce the sentence. We know that the remedy by financial compensation may cause new difficulties, because the proceedings in which victims claim financial damages can become too long again or, as in the *Pinto* cases, the compensation will be too low. So would it not be possible for the Court to say that in those cases, the only effective remedy is a preventive remedy like the one planned in Germany with the *Untätigkeitsbeschwerde*? This would be something different because it is more preventive.

N. Matz-Lück: I am very much in favour of many of these pragmatic approaches. I think they are not only relevant for length of procedure cases but more generally to cope with the workload and the backlog. I'd like to comment on two issues: the grouping of committee cases on the one hand and the threshold of dividing important from unimportant cases on the other. In your presentation you mentioned as a caveat the trust the judges would need in their law clerks if they only received a list of cases that doesn't state the facts and arguments but merely the recommended result. I think in principle you need to have trust in the legal staff at courts like the ECtHR or the Federal Constitutional Court of Germany. In any case you need to trust your law clerks in preparing the cases in a way you can quickly decide. Otherwise, it is impossible to cope with the materials of the cases. In my opinion decreasing the workload by grouping committee cases involves the balancing of effectiveness and core legal principles. You must simplify the procedure but the judges must be in the position to truly decide on the cases. If you simplify the procedure in a way that the Judge cannot fully control or check what the legal staff has actually considered, one must raise the question of legitimacy and credibility of the Court. I know from the two years in which I was working for a Judge of the Federal Constitutional Court that there were cases that were so clearly inadmissible, every word written about them seemed a waste of time. But at the other extreme, you would raise the very cynical question that if a Judge only gets a list stating that all the cases were inadmissible, why should he or she then perform the merely formal act of signing it? Why then not have the legal staff of the Registry sign the cases themselves? This consideration, of course, would be the very cynical result of a misbalancing in favour of decreasing the workload.

Concerning the threshold of dividing important cases from unimportant cases, I consider a division as absolutely essential. However, this will raise criticism in regard to the question of how to divide, i.e. how to develop criteria for distinguishing between cases. Your example was very clear: in a case where the widow of the claimant fights for several years for 50 € in compensation in a civil litigation everyone would agree it was unimportant and I agree. Furthermore, I am convinced that a large number of cases is comparable to this example and that the Court shouldn't busy itself with decisions on them. But still we have to keep in mind that for the individual applicant, his or her case is the most important and, in fact, the only important one in the world. As a consequence I am sure any decision on how to distinguish cases will raise a significant amount of criticism. At the same time I think that the development of a threshold is the essential work of the Court and it is the function of the Court to use its discretion wisely to distinguish between important and unimportant cases on an individual basis.

C. Westerdiek: Thank you *Mark [Villiger]* for your well-balanced survey pointing to the problems of the Court, the statistics and the contribution of Article 6 cases to the Court's caseload. It reminds me that as early as in March 1999, the Court set up a Working Party on Working Methods with a general mandate to rationalise the Court's working methods while at the same time maintaining legal certainty and quality of judgments. There were fundamental changes concerning for example the assignment of Registry lawyers to cases, the new principle being that national lawyers should work on the cases coming from their own legal background, the simplified processing of repetitive cases or the idea that inadmissible cases should in principle be examined by a Committee. These and the later changes in working methods enhanced productivity gains which can be seen in the Court's statistics. As not only Committee cases are grouped, but also clone/repetitive Chamber cases, Sections may deal for example with more than 100 length of proceedings or non-execution of final judgment cases on the basis of a note and a table listing the bare minimum of information on the domestic proceedings. All these reflections take place under the pressure of the ever increasing caseload and backlog of delayed applications. Because after all, with all internal improvements, applications directed in particular against the high case count countries cannot be dealt with in an acceptable period of time. And at that point, I would like to address a new development placing a burden on the Registry and the Court, which cannot be "delayed": systematic requests for the adoption of interim measures under Rule 39 of the Rules of Court in expulsion cases, a new type of "repetitive" cases. They cannot wait to be dealt with next week or next month. The comparison of the Court figures for 2006 and 2007 gives an idea about the dimension of work in dealing with these requests. Last year there were altogether 350 Rule 39 requests, of which roughly 50 were granted. We had this year already 700 requests, of which 200 were granted. The cases are mainly coming from the United Kingdom and from France and the countries of destination are mainly Sri Lanka and Somalia. Handling of these requests blocks lawyers on a daily basis, they cannot do anything else. Apart from the national lawyers, the deputy section registrars, Judge rapporteurs and the presidents of these sections are involved in this very high number of cases. And now that Christmas time is coming, the Council as usual closes down until the New Year, something we call a "duty roster" is organised where some member of staff has to check the incoming emails and faxes and the handling of any serious problems must be ensured. The problem here lies in the repetitiveness of urgent situations.

T. Marauhn: It has become clear during our discussions that there is no single and thus perfect way to address the existing problems of the European human rights system; definitely, there is not a doctrinally convincing solution. Thus, I very much appreciate the pragmatic approach taken by Judge *Villiger* in his presentation. Indeed, it seems that what we really need is a lot of pragmatism. Such pragmatism sometimes may leave us, as academics, slightly puzzled, but there are good reasons for it to be acceptable. We have to realize and to recognize that the law is not a hermetically sealed, doctrinally intelligent system but that it is designed to deal with real problems in real life. This allows me to take up two issues which are really important. The first issue concerns the prioritizing of cases. This is not just useful but important. If this is expanded further – as Mr. *Meyer-Ladewig* has already indicated –, this inserts a grain of discretionary power into handling cases. I agree with *Jochen Frowein* that, as long as we have reasonable and legitimate criteria for distinguishing between those cases which are prioritized and others which aren't, this is not only a legitimate but also a lawful approach to deal with the problem of scarce resources. A second issue which I think is very important and which could probably be developed further is the encouragement of friendly settlements. Almost all municipal court systems across the world have had problems in civil procedure because of an overload of cases. Thus, the question arises why not to introduce elements of mediation, conciliation and friendly settlement on the basis of the law as it stands. This may need some pragmatic handling. However, if it does not achieve the desired results, one might consider introducing compulsory friendly settlement, before the case is actually dealt with by the Court. I think that such an approach might be useful in particular if one follows what was outlined by Ms. *Wittling-Vogel*. This will at least reduce the number of claims. In the long run, there may be something like small claims courts in the Strasbourg system.

J. Polakiewicz: Thank you *Mark* [*Villiger*] for your very interesting presentation, which in fact shows that the Court is already doing practically everything it can do within the existing conventional system in a very pragmatic and successful way. I would like to add one more proposal to your list and make one observation. The proposal is indeed not my proposal, but that of Professor *Stephen Greer*, who unfortunately could not be with us today. In his book, which is quite thought-provoking, he made this proposal precisely for Article 6 cases, not only length of proceedings cases. He said we might need a European Fair Trials Commission, some of which could be conceived on the model of the Venice Commission. A group of practitioners in the first place and of course also professors, who would try to identify more precisely the fair trial guarantees, formulating general principles. Because what we have is the Court's case law, but this is very often too closely related to the facts of the case. It is not always easy for practitioners to identify the underlying general principles. Moreover, you have the distinction between the continental and the common law systems. Some of the Court's principles were developed more with regard to the English common law. Sometimes it is not so easy to transpose the lessons drawn from theses cases directly to a continental system.

Professor *Greer's* idea is to have an expert body, a commission, which could identify general principles without having to wait for the Court getting the right application to do this. I think there is big demand, particularly also regarding issues such as terrorism and the impact of anti-terror legislation on fair trial guarantees. I think there would be a lot to do for such a commission. What would you think about it?

My second point joins what has just been said by *Thilo* [*Marauhn*] and others. I think with this prioritizing of cases we come in fact very close to an admission procedure. If this means in practice, given the huge backlog of cases, that other cases will be dealt with at a time when the applicant no longer has any interest in the matter or may even be dead, then we are very close to Professor *Bernhardt's* scenario without a formal amendment to the Convention. There may be good reasons to proceed this way. Professor *Frowein* thinks this would be quite legitimate. I may add that the Committee of Ministers also gives priority, as far as the execution is concerned, to cases concerning structural or systemic problems. But this means that we could practically have a major reform through judicial practice alone. This is an interesting perspective and I would like to have your views about it.

C. Grabenwarter: *Mark Villiger* has addressed a number of topics. I would like to concentrate on the measures that can be taken on a national level. Measures at national level are of particular importance when it comes to problems concerning Article 6. As Ms. *Wittling-Vogel* has mentioned already, there will always be a number of applicants who will go to Strasbourg because they want to have a change of decisions which on a national level were last instance decisions. Furthermore, we must be aware that of course the reality in Europe is diverse. There are States in which applicants have more reason to go to Strasbourg than in others. This cannot be written in a legal text, but President *Wildhaber* mentioned it when he said: we do not have only democracies, real democracies, in the Council of Europe. If we turn to measures on a national level, there is the suggestion of a new convention on domestic remedies. I would agree with those who are sceptical and add one further reason why one should not pursue this idea. I am sure that we would create two classes of Member States, those who ratify this new convention and those who do not. The advantage of the fact that the Court develops standards is that all Member States are bound, whether they like it or not. It did so until the *Scordino* judgment of the Grand Chamber, where a combination of preventive and *ex post* remedies was required. Once a new convention is open for ratifications, we can see that there will be a certain danger that not all Member States will ratify it. Protocol No. 7 is a warning example. For me this is the main reason why it is not desirable to think of a new convention.

This brings me to my crucial point. I would suggest that the big majority of national courts as well as of national highest courts are willing to follow the Strasbourg case law without reservation. However, this is not always an easy task, as the example of the case law on fair hearing in matters of public service shows. In 1999, in the case of *Pellegrin v. France*, the ECtHR delivered a landmark decision on the applicability of Article 6 on disputes in the field of public service. After some hesitation, the Austrian Constitutional Court expressly followed the Strasbourg Court in September 2006, quoting *in extenso* the *Pellegrin* judgment of the European Court. Only a few months earlier the Grand Chamber judgment in the case of *Martinie* had confirmed *Pellegrin*. Only a few months later the Constitutional Court was faced with the *Eskelinen* case where the Strasbourg Court abandoned more or less the "functional approach". Instead, two new criteria were established. Let me just say that the task of Constitutional Courts in Member States – bearing in mind their limited capacities to overlook the entire case law of the Strasbourg Court – to take decisions which are in line with the case law of the ECtHR is made more difficult under these circumstances.

J.A. Frowein: Could you say a word about *Eskelinen*. Not everybody may be familiar with it.

C. Grabenwarter: The case concerned eight Finnish policemen who brought actions against a reduction of their wages. The new line in the Strasbourg case law now is that applicability does not depend any more on the task a civil servant fulfils. In order for the respondent State to be able to rely before the Court on the applicant's status as a civil servant in excluding the protection embodied in Article 6, two conditions must now be fulfilled: firstly, the State in its national law must have expressly excluded access to a court for the post or category of staff in question. Secondly, the exclusion must be justified on objective grounds in the State's interest. The mere fact that the applicant is in a sector or department which participates in the exercise of power conferred by public law is not in itself decisive. There was a large majority in the Grand Chamber. However, Mr. *Wildhaber* and Mr. *Costa* were dissenters in this case. I would like to briefly add a concluding remark, that it might reduce the workload of the Strasbourg Court if it gave more precise guidelines to national courts to follow in Article 6 cases.

L. Wildhaber: I cannot really give you a good interpretation of the majority view in *Eskelinen*. I opposed the judgment above all for reasons of judicial policy. It reminds me of the angry protest of the 1930s by a Judge in the US Supreme Court, who said that apparently the judgments of the Court were like a railroad ticket good for one day and for one distance only. I was quite opposed to changing the existing case law.

P. Mahoney: I would like to take up a point Mr. *Polakiewicz* made by putting a question to *Mark Villiger*, the question being whether it is conceivable to use this idea of prioritizing applications so as to arrive in effect at what Professor *Bernhardt* was advocating. For example, in the event of a judgment of principle holding that, as shown by accumulated findings in previous cases, unreasonable length of legal proceedings in a given country is a generalised phenomenon because of the way in which the judicial system is operated and not because of "accidents" in particular cases, would it be feasible to prioritize *negatively* length of proceedings cases from that country? That is to say, to relegate them to the bottom of the list, so that they would not be dealt with for years or even at all. If such a policy were publicly known, that might discourage lawyers from pleading the issue of length of proceedings. On the other hand, is it desirable for the ECtHR to deliberately delay the examination of applications that are raising a probably justified allegation of violation of the Convention?

Claudia Westerdiek indicated that, at the very beginning in the new Court, a whole series of practical approaches were examined. This was one of them. At the time, it was thought that as a matter of judicial policy it would not be desirable to use prioritizing in such a manner in relation to length of proceedings cases. Can one deduce that there may now be, as with the *Pellegrin* judgment on civil servants and fair trial, reexamination of a previous precedent?

I will finish with an anecdote. I once personally profited from a length of proceedings case. I have a friend in Strasbourg who is a surgeon. He phoned me one day to ask for advice on an application that he had lodged with the European Commission of Human Rights. He wanted to open a private clinic in Strasbourg and had initially been granted authorization by the competent French administrative authorities. However, all the other clinics opposed the application before the local Administrative Court. In his view, a kind of cartel trying to stifle competition for base economic reasons. My surgeon friend lost his case on appeal. He complained to me: "It is scandalous that people can use the law to block the economic freedom of their potential competitors. This is why I brought my case before the European Commission of Human Rights." I replied: "I cannot give you any advice because your case might eventually be referred to the Court." He responded: "Not so. My application has been declared inadmissible except for one single complaint about the length of the proceedings before the French administrative courts." In other words, a typical fourth-instance case of the kind that Ms. *Wittling-Vogel* referred to, with 101 complaints under Article 6 and all declared inadmissible except the one concerning length of proceedings. My friend asked: "What can I do? Can I appeal against this decision?" His reaction on receiving a negative answer was: "Oh well, then I'll forget my application. I'm personally not interested in the length of proceedings aspect; this was merely a complaint which my lawyer inserted into the application. What got me angry is the fact that the law can be used in this way to block honest initiatives by people. I'll just drop the whole thing." "Don't do that," I said. "If the complaint has been declared admissible, that means that the Commission *prima facie* considers that a violation has occurred. You will probably be receiving an offer of financial compensation from the French government, a friendly-settlement offer. You should maintain your application." Sure enough, he received his offer, he accepted it and, on the proceeds, he invited me for a very nice meal in an excellent restaurant in Strasbourg – a meal paid for by the French taxpayer. This shows, in my opinion, the ridiculous results that are too often arrived at under the Convention system as it is presently operated – because there had been a violation of the guarantee of trial within a reasonable time; and the applicant was entitled to compensation, as required by the sanctity of the right of individual petition. But what does such logic produce in practice? A three-star meal for myself and my friend. I do not believe that that is what the Strasbourg Court is there for, quite frankly.

Another point. Someone put the question: "What can national authorities do about calculating the appropriate compensation for unreasonable length of legal proceedings? Can they obtain advice from the Court?" The Court inherited from the Commission a table for awarding just satisfaction in Italian length of proceedings cases. This table, on the basis of the number of levels of jurisdiction involved and the number of years that the proceedings had lasted, indicated a figure. The Italian government asked if they could be supplied with a copy of the table. "We cannot do that," the Registry replied." It's an internal document. But you can work it out for yourself by looking at the judgments so far delivered. It's not difficult." So the Italian government did. They elaborated their own table. As soon as a plausible application on length of proceedings was communicated to the Italian government, they would immediately make a friendly-settlement offer. This offer would be made before the application had been declared admissible.

You may say that this is a very efficient way of processing cases, but it still took up an enormous amount of time and consumed enormous resources. Again, I am not sure that the performance of this kind of repetitive, mechanical, low-level judicial activity is why the Contracting States decided to set up an international Court in Strasbourg. The radical solution that I would advocate is to remove the systematic award of just satisfaction from the remit of the Strasbourg Court. Instead, award only a symbolic amount at international level, except for exceptional cases, and transfer the giving and calculation of financial compensation, especially for these repetitive cases, elsewhere – back to the national level, to be precise, on the basis of the principle of subsidiarity. I suspect that the impossibility of recovering substantial compensation at international level would have an appreciable effect on the desire of many applicants to get justice in Strasbourg. This is admittedly a radical solution, likely to have most of the NGOs up in arms protesting that it involves a denial of justice, but it would bring the Strasbourg Court back to a position where it is able to fulfil its core mission.

M. Villiger: As regards the observation by Professor *Frowein*, I think there was a misunderstanding. Of course, I agree that the principle of the equality of applicants would not be called in question if one puts cases on the fast track. Or put it this way: this is one element of many to be considered. Professor *Marauhn* has also replied to this point: precisely because there must be some sort of equality among the incoming cases, we must have legitimate reasons for prioritising. We cannot just arbitrarily say that certain applicants have priority and others not. It should be possible to fast-track, though the Court will have to work out further criteria in this respect. At the end of the day, the limits of fast-tracking would be that the Court should not prioritise more cases than it can deal with. There must always be room for the so-called less important cases to have a chance to be dealt with. If of the 50.000 cases which are filed with the Court every year, 30.000 are put on the fast track, and the Court can only deal with 30.000 a year, we would in my view have a problem.

As regards the statement by Ms. *Wittling-Vogel*, I would say that there is a very good co-operation between the Agent of the German government and the Court in matters of friendly settlements. I have before me the unilateral declaration in the most recent case of the applicant *Hassdenteufel v. Germany*, which is, I think, helpful for all parties concerned. The government accepted that the length of the proceedings was incompatible with the requirements of the Convention, and offered 6.300 € as a form of friendly settlement. The applicant did not agree, and now the Court accepts, so to say, in the name of the applicant. The problem is of course that there must be an intention by the government behind such unilateral declarations eventually to bring about legislation which does away with the potential Convention violations lying at the basis of such unilateral declarations. The Court cannot constantly accept unilateral declarations, if the envisaged revision of legislation never comes about.

As regards the statement by Mr. *Meyer-Ladewig*, just as you agree with me, I could not agree more with you.

Mr. *Milner*, as regards the alleged guidelines on amounts to be paid in friendly settlements. The applicant asks for 3 million €, but the Court awards 3.000 €. How does the Court ensure that all applicants in the same situation are treated equally? Whether or not the Court has such guidelines, or tables, as to friendly settlement-amounts, is a confidential matter. If such tables exist at all, it would for this reason not be possible to disclose them to the applicants. Now, would it be a good idea to have such guidelines, to publish them, and to tell the parties: this is what you can ask for, and no more? Maybe. It would require further discussion.

A further participant inquired about the condition of the effectiveness of remedies. The Convention says nothing on this, one has to look at the Court's case law, where you can find many indications which give substantial profile to this condition.

As regards the observation by Ms. *Peters*. For many years I have been proposing a sort of Article 41-window whereby the Court, when awarding just satisfaction, should examine whether "the internal law of the High Contracting Party concerned allows only partial reparation to be made". This would enable the Court to exercise a sort of supervision on how States react to its judgments – and in particular to see, whether *restitutio in integrum* is at all possible, and, if so, to what extent it has occurred. But the Court has done so only in very few situations, and clearly, judges are not keen to go into this matter which – this seems to be the general view – actually pertains to the Committee of Ministers of the Council of Europe. So my proposal is not for tomorrow. But I do think that in the long run one should open this window under Article 41.

Ms. *Matz*, you raise the issue of trust in lawyers by judges. This is very much a matter of experience; it also has a cultural dimension. Of course, judges trust Registry lawyers in particular as to their presentation of the facts of a case. However, a case can be made out for a Judge wishing to find out him- or herself about the basic and individual facts of a case. The Judge may wish to obtain a more immediate view as to whether or not the case is admissible and whether or not it is well-founded. But the difficulty lies in the 41 languages with which judges are confronted. It is impossible for them to examine the facts of a case in a language with they do not understand.

As regards the statement by Ms. *Westerdiek, Claudia*, we have with Professor *Frowein* shared many years in the Commission's Secretariat. Originally, in the Commission we lawyers were proud that we could deal with cases originating from all Member States. We were *polyvalent*, so to say. We were very proud of that. Eventually, as the work-load increased, Secretariat lawyers, and now lawyers of the Court's Registry, are instructed to deal only with cases from their own jurisdiction. The reason for this is, of course, that lawyers work much more efficiently when they are dealing with their own legal order. As regards duty rosters for urgent cases, I have a personal memory: I was sitting in the Court's offices in the evening of a 27th December and looking through faxes coming. I came across the urgent case of a Senegalese family about to be expelled from a Contracting State. They asked for immediate help. There I was sitting alone in my office, the building was otherwise closed, and I had to ask myself: what do I do now? How can you help these applicants! Luckily we had such a duty roster, luckily we had contact addresses in the ministries of the various Contracting States, and I could bring the case to the attention of the ministry concerned.

To the statement of Professor *Marauhn* I have already replied. Could we make friendly settlements compulsory by means of unilateral declarations? In a way, we are currently doing that in selected cases, but, as I have just pointed out, there are limits. Applicants should be aware: this is as much as they will get.

Mr. *Polakiewicz* suggested a Commission which in my view would somewhat resemble the Venice Commission. Such a Commission should decide on certain Article 6-issues. To some extent, you have yourself already replied to your question: Article 6-issues are often very much situated in the circumstances of a particular case. And when reading these judgments it will often require a considerable mental effort to extract the general principles, precisely because the facts are limited to the particular case. But of course, anything that would help the Court would be looked at very carefully.

As regards the observation by Judge *Grabenwarter, Christoph*, indeed, changes in the Strasbourg Court's case law are often difficult to digest for the domestic authorities, in particular the national courts. But what are the alternatives? Should one prohibit the Strasbourg Court from changing its case law? Hardly! Did the Court in the case of *Pellegrin v. France* not reflect sufficiently carefully when it modified its case law? Hardly! As you yourself pointed out, the Court spent many pages explaining the reasons why, how and to what extent it came to qualify its previous case law. Also, substantial changes in the case law are actually quite rare. And quite personally, I found the changes which you mentioned rather useful.

As regards the statement by Mr. *Mahoney, Paul*, of course, some Contracting States might not be happy if their cases are put on the slow track. Others, to the contrary, could be quite content with this, as it would mean that their cases would not be dealt with so quickly. This will be a further point to be kept in mind. Actually, I don't think that the issue arises in this blunt form. It would be out of question for the Court to fast- or slow-track cases originating solely from a particular country. What the Court would do – if this does not contradict the Convention, a matter which is currently being examined – would be to examine whether certain types of cases merit fast-tracking. And of course, these cases would stem from all the Contracting States.

Paul [Mahoney], your example, which is more of an anecdote, is actually somewhat cynical. Just satisfaction, in particular for immaterial damage, is awarded in respect of the applicant's suffering in the case of a breach of the Convention. The amount of money is awarded on an equitable basis and corresponds with the suffering which the applicant endured. Now, you mentioned how the particular applicant whom you knew spent this money together with you in a three-star-restaurant. Isn't it up to every applicant him- or herself to decide how this money should be spent? In fact, this applicant who spent the money in the restaurant did so upon *your* advice. If this is the way in which the person wants to overcome the suffering, well, as far as I'm concerned, that's up to the person concerned! I don't think we can call in question the whole institution of just satisfaction merely on account of the manner in which the applicant whom you know used the money awarded in the sense which you suggested to him. But let me nevertheless attempt to establish common ground between you and me. Determining amounts of just satisfaction requires a lot of time, this drains valuable resources which the Court could invest otherwise. It goes too far to propose doing away with just satisfaction, but I think the idea behind the Wise Persons' proposal – to outsource this decision – has some merits. The question is, however, to whom should the award of just satisfaction be outsourced. Should this be the national authorities, as proposed by the Wise Persons? My own personal view is that the Committee of Ministers of the Council of Europe would be very qualified for this task.

Concluding Remarks

Rüdiger Wolfrum

Thank you very much, Judge *Villiger*. It falls upon me now to make some concluding remarks which I will divide into two parts. First, I will try to summarize what we have heard and then I will make some remarks about how to proceed from here.

First of all, as I understand the presentations and the discussions over these two days, I see the possibility to identify five different approaches to the problem, which has been explained in the introduction of Professor *Frowein* and in great detail by Judge *Villiger*, at the end.

I would qualify the first approach as seeking remedies on the level of the Registry of the ECtHR. In my view seven proposals go into this direction. Another approach pursued by Professor *Bernhardt* and President *Wildhaber* tries to find a solution on the level of the Human Rights Court itself. There were also voices attempting to seek a solution on a different level, either additionally or exclusively. To put it into a nutshell, this latter approach seeks to find a solution on the national level by strengthening national procedures, making applications to the Court less likely and less frequent. Judge *Villiger* referred to this approach and so did Professor *Frowein* and Professor *Grabenwarter*. The discussion on this approach was rather controversial. Some argued that the better the national procedures are, the lesser applications should make it to the Human Rights Court. Professor *Keller*, however, objected to that view pointing out that one could look upon this approach procedurally or from a factual point of view. As a matter of fact, I would assume that the better the national procedure is, the fewer applications should be made to Strasbourg. Whether this fact may be reflected procedurally is a different question. The fourth approach I would see is a combination of the former three. It was brought into the discussion by Ms. *Seibert-Fohr* particularly when she mentioned the combination of this national procedure and the proposal that has been made by Professor *Bernhardt*.

There was, however, a fifth approach and here I saw most controversies. It was the idea of *Armin von Bogdandy* to involve the new European Union Agency for Fundamental Rights. Some were in favour of this proposal, others were rather vigorously against it for several reasons, including the limited functions of this Agency. I would add that the agency may lack the necessary independence. Mr. *Polakiewicz*, however, mentioned a fair trial commission as one additional option, a proposal which might lead into the same direction.

I don't think we have found the perfect solution. Nobody expected us to be wiser than the wise. I believe, however, that we have identified the problems, indicated some avenues for further thoughts and perhaps laid a groundwork for further considerations.

Let me thank you very much, first for coming; I realise that for some it was an awkward period of the year, so shortly before Christmas. I also thank you in advance for your cooperation in putting the manuscript together. And finally, I would like to express my gratitude to the staff and Mr. *Saw* in particular, on whose shoulders the whole administration and preparation rested and the follow-up will be and to Ms. *Klein*, who helped him and me in every respect most efficiently.

List of Participants

Bernhardt, Rudolf
Max Planck Institute for Comparative Public Law and International Law

von Bernstorff, Jochen
Max Planck Institute for Comparative Public Law and International Law

Beyerlin, Ulrich
Max Planck Institute for Comparative Public Law and International Law

von Bogdandy, Armin
Director at the Max Planck Institute for Comparative Public Law and International Law

Doehring, Karl
Max Planck Institute for Comparative Public Law and International Law

Forowicz, Magdalena
University of Zurich, Faculty of Law

Frowein, Jochen Abr.
Max Planck Institute for Comparative Public Law and International Law

Grabenwarter, Christoph
Karl-Franzens-Universität, Graz, Institut für Österreichisches, Europäisches und Vergleichendes Öffentliches Recht

Greer, Stephen
University of Bristol, School of Law

Grote, Rainer
Max Planck Institute for Comparative Public Law and International Law

Hess, Burkhard
Dekan der Juristischen Fakultät, Ruprecht-Karls-Universität Heidelberg

Hoffmeister, Frank
European Commission, Legal Service

Hofmann, Rainer
Johann Wolfgang Goethe-Universität Frankfurt, Lehrstuhl für Öffentliches Recht, Völker- und Europarecht

Keller, Helen
University of Zurich, Faculty of Law

Kühne, Daniela
University of Zurich, Faculty of Law

Less, Steven
Max Planck Institute for Comparative Public Law and International Law

Macalister-Smith, Peter
Max Planck Institute for Comparative Public Law and International Law

Mahoney, Paul
President of the European Union Civil Service Tribunal

List of Participants

Marauhn, Thilo
Justus-Liebig-Universität Giessen, Fachbereich Rechtswissenschaft

Matz-Lück, Nele
Max Planck Institute for Comparative Public Law and International Law

Meyer-Ladewig, Jens
Ministerialdirigent a.D., Bundesministerium der Justiz

Milner, David
Council of Europe, Human Rights Intergovernmental Cooperation Division

Morales Antoniazzi, Mariela
Max Planck Institute for Comparative Public Law and International Law

Müller, Reinhard
Political Editor, Frankfurter Allgemeine Zeitung

Oellers-Frahm, Karin
Max Planck Institute for Comparative Public Law and International Law

Oeter, Stefan
Institut für Internationale Angelegenheiten, Fakultät für Rechtswissenschaft, Universität Hamburg

de Oliveira Godinho, Fabiana
Max Planck Institute for Comparative Public Law and International Law

Peters, Anne
Ordinaria für Völker- und Staatsrecht, Universität Basel, Juristische Fakultät

Petzold, Herbert
Former Registrar of the European Court of Human Rights

Pichon, Jakob
Max Planck Institute for Comparative Public Law and International Law

Polakiewicz, Jörg
Council of Europe, Directorate General of Human Rights – DG II

Puma, Giuseppe
University of Rome La Sapienza

Ress, Georg
Jacobs University Bremen, Former Judge of the European Court of Human Rights

Ruedin, Xavier
University of Bern

Saw, Falilou
Max Planck Institute for Comparative Public Law and International Law

Schmalenbach, Kirsten
Universität Graz, Institut für Völkerrecht und internationale Beziehungen

List of Participants

Seibert-Fohr, Anja
Max Planck Institute for Comparative Public Law and International Law

Smrkolj, Maja
Max Planck Institute for Comparative Public Law and International Law

Steinberger, Helmut
Max Planck Institute for Comparative Public Law and International Law

Tomuschat, Christian
Humboldt-Universität zu Berlin, Institut für Völker- und Europarecht

Villiger, Mark
Former President of the European Court of Human Rights

Vöneky, Silja
Max Planck Institute for Comparative Public Law and International Law

Weber, Anne
Max Planck Institute for Comparative Public Law and International Law

Westerdiek, Claudia
Registry, European Court of Human Rights

de Wet, Erika
University of Amsterdam, Faculty of Law, Department of International Law

Wildhaber, Luzius
Former President of the European Court of Human Rights

Wittling-Vogel, Almut
Ministerialdirigentin, Beauftragte der Bundesregierung für Menschenrechtsfragen, Bundesministerium der Justiz

Wolfrum, Rüdiger
Director at the Max Planck Institute for Comparative Public Law and International Law

Zacharias, Diana
Max Planck Institute for Comparative Public Law and International Law

Max-Planck-Institut für ausländisches öffentliches Recht und Völkerrecht

Beiträge zum ausländischen öffentlichen Recht und Völkerrecht

Hrsg.: A. von Bogdandy, R. Wolfrum

Bde. 27–59 erschienen im Carl Heymanns Verlag KG Köln, Berlin (Bestellung an: Max-Planck-Institut für Völkerrecht, Im Neuenheimer Feld 535, 69120 Heidelberg); ab Band 60 im Springer-Verlag Berlin, Heidelberg, New York, London, Paris, Tokyo, Hong Kong, Barcelona

---

205 Rüdiger *Wolfrum*, Ulrike *Deutsch* (eds.): **The European Court of Human Rights Overwhelmed by Applications: Problems and Possible Solutions.** 2009. VIII, 128 Seiten. Geb. € 59,95 zzgl. landesüblicher MwSt.

204 Niels *Petersen*: **Demokratie als teleologisches Prinzip.** 2009. XXVII, 280 Seiten. Geb. € 79,95

203 Christiane *Kamardi*: **Die Ausformung einer Prozessordnung sui generis durch das ICTY unter Berücksichtigung des Fair-Trial-Prinzips.** 2009. XVI, 424 Seiten. Geb. € 89,95

202 Leonie F. *Guder*: **The Administration of Debt Relief by the International Financial Institutions.** 2009. XVIII, 355 Seiten. Geb. € 84,95 zzgl. landesüblicher MwSt.

201 Silja *Vöneky*, Cornelia *Hagedorn*, Miriam *Clados*, Jelena *von Achenbach*: **Legitimation ethischer Entscheidungen im Recht.** 2009. VIII, 351 Seiten. Geb. € 84,95

200 Anja Katarina *Weilert*: **Grundlagen und Grenzen des Folterverbotes in verschiedenen Rechtskreisen.** 2009. XXX, 474 Seiten. Geb. € 94,95

199 Suzette V. *Suarez*: **The Outer Limits of the Continental Shelf.** 2008. XVIII, 276 Seiten. Geb. € 79,95 zzgl. landesüblicher MwSt.

198 Felix *Hanschmann*: **Der Begriff der Homogenität in der Verfassungslehre und Europarechtswissenschaft.** 2008. XIII, 370 Seiten. Geb. € 84,95

197 Angela *Paul*: **Kritische Analyse und Reformvorschlag zu Art. II Genozidkonvention.** 2008. XVI, 379 Seiten. Geb. € 84,95

196 Hans Fabian *Kiderlen*: **Von Triest nach Osttimor.** 2008. XXVI, 526 Seiten. Geb. € 94,95

195 Heiko *Sauer*: **Jurisdiktionskonflikte in Mehrebenensystemen.** 2008. XXXVIII, 605 Seiten. Geb. € 99,95

194 Rüdiger *Wolfrum*, Volker *Röben* (eds.): **Legitimacy in International Law.** 2008. VI, 420 Seiten. Geb. € 84,95 zzgl. landesüblicher MwSt.

193 Doris *König*, Peter-Tobias *Stoll*, Volker *Röben*, Nele *Matz-Lück* (eds.): **International Law Today: New Challenges and the Need for Reform?** 2008. VIII, 260 Seiten. Geb. € 69,95 zzgl. landesüblicher MwSt.

192 Ingo *Niemann*: **Geistiges Eigentum in konkurrierenden völkerrechtlichen Vertragsordnungen.** 2008. XXV, 463 Seiten. Geb. € 94,95

191 Nicola *Wenzel*: **Das Spannungsverhältnis zwischen Gruppenschutz und Individualschutz im Völkerrecht.** 2008. XXXI, 646 Seiten. Geb. € 99,95

190 Winfried *Brugger*, Michael *Karayanni* (eds.): **Religion in the Public Sphere: A Comparative Analysis of German, Israeli, American and International Law.** 2007. XVI, 467 Seiten. Geb. € 89,95 zzgl. landesüblicher MwSt.

189 Eyal *Benvenisti*, Chaim *Gans*, Sari *Hanafi* (eds.): **Israel and the Palestinian Refugees.** 2007. VIII, 502 Seiten. Geb. € 94,95 zzgl. landesüblicher MwSt.

188 Eibe *Riedel*, Rüdiger *Wolfrum* (eds.): **Recent Trends in German and European Constitutional Law.** 2006. VII, 289 Seiten. Geb. € 74,95 zzgl. landesüblicher MwSt.

187 Marcel *Kau*: **United States Supreme Court und Bundesverfassungsgericht.** 2007. XXV, 538 Seiten. Geb. € 99,95 zzgl. landesüblicher MwSt.

186 Philipp *Dann*, Michał *Rynkowski* (eds.): **The Unity of the European Constitution.** 2006. IX, 394 Seiten. Geb. € 79,95 zzgl. landesüblicher MwSt.

185 Pál *Sonnevend*: **Eigentumsschutz und Sozialversicherung.** 2008. XVIII, 278 Seiten. Geb. € 74,95

184 Jürgen *Bast*: **Grundbegriffe der Handlungsformen der EU.** 2006. XXI, 485 Seiten. Geb. € 94,95

183 Uwe *Säuberlich*: **Die außervertragliche Haftung im Gemeinschaftsrecht.** 2005. XV, 314 Seiten. Geb. € 74,95

182 Florian *von Alemann*: **Die Handlungsform der interinstitutionellen Vereinbarung.** 2006. XVI, 518 Seiten. Geb. € 94,95

181 Susanne *Förster*: **Internationale Haftungsregeln für schädliche Folgewirkungen gentechnisch veränderter Organismen.** 2007. XXXVI, 421 Seiten. Geb. € 84,95

180 Jeanine *Bucherer*: **Die Vereinbarkeit von Militärgerichten mit dem Recht auf ein faires Verfahren gemäß Art. 6 Abs. 1 EMRK, Art. 8 Abs. 1 AMRK und Art. 14 Abs. 1 des UN Paktes über bürgerliche und politische Rechte.** 2005. XVIII, 307 Seiten. Geb. € 74,95

179 Annette *Simon*: **UN-Schutzzonen – Ein Schutzinstrument für verfolgte Personen?** 2005. XXI, 322 Seiten. Geb. € 74,95

178 Petra *Minnerop*: **Paria-Staaten im Völkerrecht?** 2004. XXIII, 579 Seiten. Geb. € 99,95

177 Rüdiger *Wolfrum*, Volker *Röben* (eds.): **Developments of International Law in Treaty Making.** 2005. VIII, 632 Seiten. Geb. € 99,95 zzgl. landesüblicher MwSt.

176 Christiane *Höhn*: **Zwischen Menschenrechten und Konfliktprävention. Der Minderheitenschutz im Rahmen der Organisation für Sicherheit und Zusammenarbeit in Europa (OSZE).** 2005. XX, 418 Seiten. Geb. € 84,95

175 Nele *Matz*: **Wege zur Koordinierung völkerrechtlicher Verträge. Völkervertragsrechtliche und institutionelle Ansätze.** 2005. XXIV, 423 Seiten. Geb. € 84,95

174 Jochen Abr. *Frowein*: **Völkerrecht – Menschenrechte – Verfassungsfragen Deutschlands und Europas. Ausgewählte Schriften.** Hrsg. von Matthias *Hartwig*, Georg *Nolte*, Stefan *Oeter*, Christian *Walter*. 2004. VIII, 732 Seiten. Geb. € 119,95

173 Oliver *Dörr* (Hrsg.): **Ein Rechtslehrer in Berlin. Symposium für Albrecht Randelzhofer.** 2004. VII, 117 Seiten. Geb. € 54,95

172 Lars-Jörgen *Geburtig*: **Konkurrentenrechtsschutz aus Art. 88 Abs. 3 Satz 3 EGV. Am Beispiel von Steuervergünstigungen.** 2004. XVII, 412 Seiten (4 Seiten English Summary). Geb. € 84,95

171 Markus *Böckenförde*: **Grüne Gentechnik und Welthandel. Das Biosafety-Protokoll und seine Auswirkungen auf das Regime der WTO.** 2004. XXIX, 620 Seiten. Geb. € 99,95

170 Anja *v. Hahn*: **Traditionelles Wissen indigener und lokaler Gemeinschaften zwischen geistigen Eigentumsrechten und der public domain.** 2004. XXV, 415 Seiten. Geb. 84,95

169 Christian *Walter*, Silja *Vöneky*, Volker *Röben*, Frank *Schorkopf* (eds.): **Terrorism as a Challenge for National and International Law: Security versus Liberty?** 2004. XI, 1484 Seiten. Geb. € 169,95 zzgl. landesüblicher MwSt.

168 Kathrin *Osteneck*: **Die Umsetzung von UN-Wirtschaftssanktionen durch die Europäische Gemeinschaft.** 2004. XXXIX, 579 Seiten. Geb. € 99,95

167 Stephan *Sina*: **Der völkerrechtliche Status des Westjordanlandes und des Gaza-Streifens nach den Osloer Verträgen.** 2004. XXI, 410 Seiten. Geb. € 84,95

166 Philipp *Dann*: **Parlamente im Exekutivföderalismus.** 2004. XXIII, 474 Seiten. Geb. € 89,95

165 Rüdiger *Wolfrum* (Hrsg.): **Gleichheit und Nichtdiskriminierung im nationalen und internationalen Menschenrechtsschutz.** 2003. VIII, 299 Seiten. Geb. € 74,95

164 Rüdiger *Wolfrum*, Nele *Matz*: **Conflicts in International Environmental Law.** 2003. XI, 213 Seiten. Geb. € 64,95 zzgl. landesüblicher MwSt.

163 Adam *Bodnar*, Michał *Kowalski*, Karen *Raible*, Frank *Schorkopf* (eds.): **The Emerging Constitutional Law of the European Union.** 2003. IX, 595 Seiten. Geb. € 99,95 zzgl. landesüblicher MwSt.

162 Jochen Abr. *Frowein*, Klaus *Scharioth*, Ingo *Winkelmann*, Rüdiger *Wolfrum* (Hrsg.): **Verhandeln für den Frieden/Negotiating for Peace. Liber Amicorum Tono Eitel.** 2003. XIII, 866 Seiten. Geb. € 129,95

161 Michaela *Fries*: **Die Bedeutung von Artikel 5 (f) der Rassendiskriminierungskonvention im deutschen Recht.** 2003. XIX, 429 Seiten. Geb. € 84,95

Printing: Krips bv, Meppel, The Netherlands
Binding: Stürtz, Würzburg, Germany